A FUNNY KIND OF LOVE

Siân Lloyd

A FUNNY KIND OF LOVE

My Story

JOHN BLAKE

First published in hardback in 2008

ISBN 978 1 84454 531 5

British Library Cataloguing-in-Publication Data:

A catalogue record for this book is available from the British Library.

Design by www.envydesign.co.uk

Printed in the UK by CPI William Clowes
Beccles NR34 7TL

1 3 5 7 9 10 8 6 4 2

Papers used by John Blake Publishing are natural, recyclable
products made from wood grown in sustainable forests.
The manufacturing processes conform to the environmental
regulations of the country of origin.

Every attempt has been made to contact the relevant copyright-holders,
but some were unobtainable. We would be grateful if the appropriate
people could contact us.

Thanks to Neil – without whom I couldn't have done it.
To Eileen for her help, support and amazing memory.
And to Jonathan for encouraging, prompting and inspiring
me to get my act together, and simply for being in my life.

Contents

Introduction

'Where's Lembit?'

If two words can sum up a relationship, then those two sum up ours.

And I had no idea where Lembit Opik was when my father was rushed into an intensive care ward in Wales. The moment my mother called me with the news I took myself off the weather roster at ITN. I cancelled my other work and raced along the M4 to Swansea to be with him. When I arrived, I called Lembit but I couldn't get through.

So where was he?

My mum, my brother David and I took turns by Dad's bedside. We paced up and down the waiting room and hospital corridors. And I made call after call to Lembit on my mobile. They all went unanswered. And so the hours passed.

Amazing to think of it now, but Lembit and I were engaged. The papers had been full of stories of the wedding we were supposed to be planning, but Lembit had never been around to discuss those plans. And he certainly wasn't there now when I needed him most: when my dad was fighting for his life in hospital. The whole time there was no phone call to me, no card or flowers for my father, no visit... No communication to my mum, my sister Ceri or brother David, the wonderful, generous people who always tried so hard to welcome him into our family.

So where was he? And why, really, was I surprised that he had gone to ground?

After nearly a week of unanswered calls and desperate voice messages I made my decision. The next call would be our last. I had already forgiven so much, but I couldn't forgive this. If Lembit forced me to end our four-year relationship on voicemail or by text, then he would have no one to blame but himself.

As it turned out, he did answer my final call. I was standing just outside the hospital waiting room. Doctors, nurses, patients and relatives were passing by all the time. It was the worst possible place for such an important, life-changing conversation. But with Lembit beggars can't be choosers. I had long since learned that I had to speak to him when I got him, and I had to speak fast. If ignoring my calls was his favourite party trick, then cutting me off mid-sentence in favour of someone more important came a close second. And recently all sorts of people had started to be more important than me, or so it seemed.

'Lembit, why haven't you called me back?'

I hate being a nag but I couldn't just let him brush all this under the carpet. This was about my father as much as it was about me. I owed it to my dad to be tough. Of course, he had no proper answer – meetings, missed connections, being busy, Parliamentary business, something in the constituency in Wales... All the usual excuses, none of them ever meant a thing.

'But you've had time to go on some trashy television show...' I couldn't stop myself from saying it.

My agent, Seamus, had told me that he'd had reports from people he represented about Lembit behaving outrageously at the after-show party of some new talent show. I hadn't let my father see the story; I didn't want him to know how little his prospective son-in-law appeared to think of our family.

Lembit was hundreds of miles away in London and suddenly I could tell he was smiling. He couldn't care less how trashy the show was – he was just thrilled that he had been invited on to it, and not me.

'Lembit, we have to talk,' I said, after what felt like an endless, empty silence. It was crystal clear what I meant, but it seemed as though he wanted me to put it into words. He was too weak, too much of a coward to end our relationship himself. The unanswered phone calls at such a terrible time for my family, this cold, clinical conversation today... He had closed down emotionally, just the way he always did. He was using silence to control the agenda, seeming to manipulate everything perhaps to ensure that I did the deed and got him off the hook. But suddenly I was the one to crack a short smile; suddenly I realised nothing would give me more pleasure.

From a hospital corridor in South Wales, I told Lembit we had to call off our wedding. I told him our relationship was over for good. And oh, how great that felt.

Call it karma, but my father started to recover at pretty

much the same time. In Wales, the dark clouds and everyone's grim, black moods were lifting. My wonderful mother, brother and sister all tried so hard to support me when I started dating Lembit, but they had long since stopped believing we were right for each other. They had seen all the cracks and failings I missed, and now they were euphoric that the old Siân was on her way back.

When my father was discharged from hospital, we had the most wonderful family meal back at home. It felt as if we were all being given second chances. I vowed not to spoil mine, and I couldn't stop dancing on air.

Telling my friends was as good as telling my family. When you say you've broken off your engagement and ended a four-year relationship, you expect people to say how sorry they are; you expect commiserations and concern for your welfare. None of my friends wasted time on any of that. I could practically hear champagne corks popping in the background when most of them heard that Lembit was history. They were thrilled they would never have to sit through another tense, boozy dinner party with him ever again.

Back in South Wales, I knew I had done the right thing at long last. I added it all up and realised I had given Lembit two years of extra chances after our relationship really died. Because of the deaths of his close friend Graham, his father Uno and his brother Endel, I stayed at his side for two years too long. I'm proud I didn't leave him when he was on the floor but in the process I lost two years of my own life. Now I was free. I could enjoy time on my own, and time with my wonderful friends. There was so much I still wanted to see and do in the world.

INTRODUCTION

Now the shackles were off, it felt as if there were no limits to what I could achieve.

And Lembit? He could carry on his late-night party lifestyle in London without me. He could misbehave as much as he wanted on as many TV channels as he chose. I thought back to that gossip doing the rounds about his post-show behaviour and I didn't doubt something probably happened with one of the other competitors.

I wondered idly what he might be up to. Something told me he wasn't going to go quietly. Suddenly the whole thing seemed even more bizarre. Lembit was the Liberal Democrat MP for Montgomeryshire, deep in the heart of rural Wales. He was supposed to be a credible, heavyweight party spokesperson for Wales and Northern Ireland, of all things. So why had he been messing around on something called the *All Star Talent Show*? Did he think it was clever to play the harmonica in a London television studio? And who the hell were the Cheeky Girls?

Chapter One
Welsh Women

I'm Welsh, through and through. I think that partly helped me survive the break-up with Lembit. Welsh women are a tough bunch and Welsh men are among the best around. I should never have allowed myself to be fooled by someone who lived in our country but never quite understood what it stands for. Lembit may still have a house in Newtown but I don't think Wales will ever be his true home.

My Welsh roots run deep and wide. Two generations ago, my grandfather Mel Thomas was in the pits just like everyone else. Even then my family were fighters; they didn't let the world beat them down. My grandfather was very active locally in the South Wales Miners Federation as head of the Compensation Department for pneumoconiosis, presenting the cases in court on behalf of men suffering from the illness and leading local campaigns to improve conditions in the mines. He had seen too many friends and colleagues die in gas explosions and industrial accidents, and too many become ill after spending their lives underground amid the coal dust. So he did something about it. He demanded changes, and he rose through the ranks of the National Union of Mineworkers as he fought for compensation and better conditions.

You don't hear much about the horrors of pneumoconiosis – the infamous 'numo' – and its associated illnesses today. I'm proud to think my grandfather and all the other campaigners played a huge part in that. His example has always inspired me.

At home my grandparents blazed other trails as well. They all saw education as a way for their children to make a better life. Money might be tight but whenever there was any to spare my parents say it was always spent on books. Little wonder, perhaps, both of them became teachers. That was the best way out of the mines, back then. Little wonder either that my mum, Barbara, and dad, Trevor, were both politically aware or that they passed on their social consciences when they had children of their own.

I was born in Maesteg General Hospital in Bridgend on 3 July 1958. Funnily enough, the weather made the news that day. South Wales was living through one of the biggest storms of the century. I arrived with thunder rolling through the clouds and lightning streaking across the sky.

Two years later, I got a younger sister, Ceri, and a year after that a brother, David. As the eldest of the three I grew up fast and from the start I was determined to please people. Mum called me 'a great little helper' and I loved it. I would run and fetch anything she ever needed. Old-fashioned terry towelling nappies, safety pins, talcum powder... All my early memories are suffused with the smell of talc.

My next memories are all about the books. Our house in Neath was full of them. It was a wonderful home; the kind of place that looks small from the outside but opens up like a Tardis once you get through the door. And we needed every inch of space we could find. In every room the walls were covered in shelves all stacked with books. Bright flashes of orange came from my mother's Penguins that rubbed spines with my father's outsized art books and thick tomes on economic theory.

We were taught to treasure those books as children. They were more valuable than anything else we ever owned; they opened windows to new worlds. Education was always going to be the cornerstone of our lives. No wonder Mum and Dad were so upset years later when a journalist said I was just another 'brainless' blonde weather girl.

My parents were both teachers and incredibly busy people. Mum wasn't just head of English and French at Llangatwg, she also ran the library and became national president of the National Union of Teachers. She was a campaigner through and through. And she is the ultimate proof that if you want a job doing you should give it to a busy woman.

Dad had been a history teacher, a keen hiker and a member of the local debating society. Oh, and he was a fantastic cook who made most of our meals at home. No wonder the three of us were brought up to believe that anything is possible in life. I don't think the word 'can't' was ever in the family vocabulary.

Dad had other ways to prove we should always go that extra mile – quite literally. From the time my little brother David could stand, Dad would take us three kids out for long walks across the Gower Peninsula. But we never went to any of the more accessible beaches. 'I want to go far from the madding crowd,' Dad would say, one of the many literary quotes that always swirled around us. Whenever I complained and asked for an easier option, I would get the same response: 'If it's difficult to get to the beach, there will be fewer people there when we arrive.'

He was always right and our empty beaches were always worth seeing. Equally good were the treats we would all get when we threw ourselves down on the sands. Dad brought some of the bread he baked every day in our Aga. We would tear off big hunks and cover them in lashings of salty Welsh butter from Swansea market. Add a thin layer of Marmite, some crunchy iceberg lettuce, hardboiled eggs, homemade rock cakes and scones and I reckon we had the best picnics in the country.

When it came to our schooling, Mum and Dad proved yet again that we were no ordinary family. They weren't Welsh speakers and back in the 1960s a lot of people thought the language slightly infra dig. But my parents were never going to follow conventional wisdom on this – or anything else. They decided that learning a new language would give us children an extra edge in whatever we did as adults, and they couldn't have been more right.

As the eldest, I was the first to face the challenge so I didn't just go through the usual terrors of the first day at school, I also had to face the fact that at Neath Welsh School we were only encouraged to speak English in our

English lessons. Apart from that, it was Welsh all the way. When I first arrived, I didn't know a single word of it so I had to learn fast. Luckily, I thrived on it.

Today I'm so proud I can still speak fluent Welsh. It makes me feel closer to my roots. Being bilingual also means a third or fourth language comes much more easily to me. My nephew Owen was brought up in Paris and is totally trilingual. I've never really understood why so many British people have a mental block when it comes to languages – the more the merrier as far as I'm concerned! There's another benefit too. When I'm out and about in London with other Welsh speakers, we can use it as a code to get out of boring situations. It's naughty, but useful.

At home, Mum and Dad worked hard to help my brother, sister and me with our new language. Every Saturday morning Dad would make us all listen to Hywel Gwynfryn's Welsh-language radio show. He also subscribed to the Welsh-language newspaper *Y Cymro*; it had a children's club, Clwb y Cymro, and every weekend we weren't allowed to go out and play with our friends until we had entered its essay-writing and short-story competitions. As it turned out, the competition entries weren't much of a hardship – between us, Ceri, David and I kept on winning them.

Over the years we collected lots of postal orders as prizes and even got our pictures in the local paper. When we did win, we would all pile into our black Austin 30 – to this day I remember our 0B0 60-licence plate – to drive into Swansea to spend the money. But we couldn't spend it on just anything. Clothes, sweets or other frivolities were all off limits. We went to the Ty John Penry Welsh bookshop to buy yet more books. While all this might sound a bit grim for a group of children today, we loved it. I'd rush in, desperate to see my favourite old titles and all the new stock. I'd want to buy far more than my postal orders would allow, and sometimes I would get the chance.

Bookshops were the only place where money was no object with my parents. They were thrilled that we loved reading as much as they did, so our prize money was often topped up with a little extra. Today books are still my ultimate luxury item. They were what I missed most in the jungle all those years later on *I'm A Celebrity*...

Looking back, it's clear that our parents were determined to open up as many horizons as possible for the three of us. Dad was an atheist and my mother was an agnostic, but both of them insisted we went to Bethania Chapel every Sunday afternoon. They said they wanted us to learn about religion so we could then make up our own minds about God.

For my part, Sunday school did more than just teach me about the Bible. It let me grow as a person as well – and that was all due to the buxom and charismatic Mrs O.G. Davis who led the weekly lessons. We called her Mrs O.G. and she was an extraordinary character. She was always meticulously turned out – very smart, with a big fur coat and an amazing hat. In her lessons she'd take us around the world and back, talking about different countries and customs. Then she would talk about fashion, shops and restaurants.

She'd make wonderful statements that transported me to glamorous, grown-up worlds. One week Mrs O.G. declared,

'The Kardomah in Swansea is the only place to have a coffee.' It sounded like the most sophisticated place in the world. I was desperate to visit and taste grown-up coffee.

Then there were the fashion tips. A week would never pass without us being told, 'Blue and green should never be seen,' or some such gem. My lifelong obsession with clothes began right there, though I soon became just a little bit more adventurous than Mrs O.G.

The other stories our teacher told were just as intoxicating. When I was ten, the upcoming wedding of Mrs O.G.'s daughter Eryl became a weekly serial that gripped everyone. We all knew about the flowers, the hymns, the colour of the dresses, what was going to be said at the service, absolutely everything, for Mrs O.G. wove wonderful pictures with her words. Then, in a heartbeat, she could take us back to religion, drawing out a moral lesson from what she'd said. It was incredible.

Even as a little girl in Sunday school, I realised how much it meant that Mrs O.G. talked to us about her life and her family. Today I understand that it is when people open up and volunteer details of their life that you know you have a true friend. It's so flattering when they give you their time and let you into their world. It produces a warm feeling of companionship that I think is quite a Welsh thing. To this day I'm proud when people share confidences with me, even if they are just the smallest of things. Mrs O.G. taught me the value of that. She was also the first adult outside our family to talk to me like an equal and for this – and for her friendship – I'll be eternally grateful. For me, she was the first bridge into a bigger, more adult world.

Unfortunately, I can't pretend I didn't sometimes let the great lady down. An early example came one Christmas when I was chosen to be Mary in the nativity play. My best friend Aled expected to land the role of Joseph and was very upset when he was told he was to be the innkeeper. Instead of a star part he had just one line: 'We don't have any rooms but there is a space in the barn with fresh hay.' As the weeks passed I could tell this was driving him mad. He was clearly convinced he had more to offer so on the big night itself he decided to do his own thing. When Joseph asked for a room and stood back for the much-rehearsed response, Aled thrust his arm outwards and said, 'Yes, we've got plenty of rooms. Would you like one with a view?'

As if changing the whole course of Christianity wasn't bad enough I got the giggles. I doubled up with my hands on my mouth and just couldn't stop laughing. 'Concentrate children, concentrate,' Mrs O.G. hissed to try to get the story back on to its more traditional path. And I'm sorry to say it took me longer than anyone else to calm down and let this happen.

Another bridge into the adult world came shortly after this. We had never had a television in our house – ironic for someone who would end up as a presenter, so bedtime stories were particularly important to us. I had already fallen in love with books and, as well as making up stories for them, I was always ready to read to Ceri and David. *Swallows and Amazons*, *The Borrowers*, *The Famous Five* and the *Secret Seven* books were my first favourites closely followed by all the *Just William* stories and *The Chronicles of Narnia*.

But even as a child I was always ready to move on. I think I was always in a hurry, always looking for the next step up some ladder. When I was about 10 or 11, I got on a chair so I could reach some of my mum's higher shelves. Something told me the stories up there might be more interesting, and I was right. The first I picked was *The Virgin Soldiers* by Leslie Thomas. It wasn't the title that attracted me – I didn't have a clue what a virgin was. I chose it simply because it was the highest book I could reach. It also had a broken spine. That told me it had been read already so no one would notice if I did the same.

One night when Ceri and David were asleep, I started reading. I couldn't put it down. I didn't really understand everything, but I knew that what Brigg and Juicy Lucy were doing was quite adult. I was thrilled. I finished the whole book in a matter of weeks and was soon back on that chair looking for further adventures.

My next choice was even more controversial. My hand had landed on an Edna O'Brien title called *The Country Girl*. At the time, I had no idea that the text had been considered so racy it had been banned shortly after publication in Ireland. Apparently, it had even been burned occasionally in Irish churchyards. The people doing so would probably have been horrified that some schoolgirl was lapping it all up just over the Irish Sea.

Needless to say, I loved the story. I read whole chapters in each sitting, always terrified I'd be found out, but unable to stop myself from turning the pages. Once I'd finished I was back reading even more unsuitable books. Certainly I'd come a long way from Julian, George and the rest of the Famous Five! Somehow I never got found out.

I always picked well-worn books with broken spines and made sure I put them back on the shelf carefully so my parents wouldn't spot that they had been touched.

Of course, getting away with this probably made me over-confident. I needed to be shown that parents do find things out in the end and that happened with my so-called musical career. Every Wednesday after school, I had piano lessons with Madam Winnie just a few streets away from our house. I'm not sure which of us hated the experience the most. While I could remember the notes and soon learned how to read music, I wasn't musical: I had no feeling, no rhythm. When I played piano, I was like a pet shop on fire – as my friend Stifyn Parri said many years later when he described my singing. Dear Madam Winnie tried and tried to soften my rough edges but her pained expressions told me I was the pupil from hell. I'm sure she knew far sooner than I did that I'm completely tone deaf.

One day I just couldn't face the hour-long lesson. I dawdled along the street, dragging my heels, desperate for a distraction. As usual, when I arrived I was dreaming of a million reasons why Madam Winnie might have to cancel the lesson but I knew my dreams were unlikely to come true. So, I stopped outside my favourite little shop – 'Annie's Sweetshop' – to delay my arrival for just a little longer. I was hypnotised by the jars of multicoloured sweets in the window. Next thing I knew I had opened the door. A bell rang and the scent of all that wonderful sugar hit my nose. Annie herself was smiling down at me and asking what I wanted. It would have been rude not to reply.

Minutes later I handed over my piano money in exchange for a large bag of rose and lemon Turkish delight. As soon as I got outside, I popped one of the soft pink squares into my mouth. It tasted better than any sweet I'd ever had before – illicit and extremely naughty. That night I joined the rest of the family round the dinner table and prepared to be found out. But I wasn't. And the following week, when it was time for piano again I was round to Annie's for more Turkish delight just like Edmund in *The Lion The Witch and The Wardrobe.*

After that second time, I couldn't stop. Week after week, I just skived and scoffed. Incredibly, I got away with it for three wonderful, fattening months. But then it happened: Madam Winnie phoned my dad one night just as we sat down for dinner.

'Is Siân all right?' she asked. 'I've been very concerned about her.'

The game was up. I got a real blasting from my mum and dad. It was pretty much the first time I'd ever been properly told off – and it hurt. They said I'd betrayed their trust and been a snake in the grass, that I should be ashamed of myself and that I'd let everybody down. That last line was the one that really got me: I was the good girl, I didn't disappoint people. I was so overcome with remorse I even said I would have piano lessons every day to catch up. Possibly a horrified Madam Winnie knocked that idea on the head. Anyway, my musical career seemed to be over. I didn't have another rose and lemon Turkish Delight for a long time either. Every time I do, I think about Big Annie, Madam Winnie and the night I let my parents down.

However busy Mum was with school, the union work and her new political campaigns, she always made sure she sat down with us each night to eat and to talk. We had a great kitchen. Our big cream, coal-fired Aga dominated the room. We had two cats that were always lying around it – a Siamese called Siamese and a beautiful Persian called Catrin. And then there was the big family table we always sat around. The table and chairs were all handcrafted Ercol; the chairs had tweed check on their cushions, a subtle blend of brown, black and beige. They had been an expensive buy for my parents but my mother loved them.

'They'll be the antiques of the future,' she used to say. She had a good eye and she was right. She's the reason I love to buy art and furniture today.

Mum's specialities were corned beef pie and lemon meringue tart. Dad's cooking was wonderful, though it wasn't for the faint-hearted. He would serve up oxtail casseroles, pork bellies and even roast stuffed hearts. Dad also ruled the room and made us all eat up everything we were given. One time David was caught throwing his hated spinach on to the floor. Dad made him stay at the table for hours until he finally ate what was left of it. Fussy eating was never really an option for us kids; we knew we had to do as we were told.

So were we just another totally typical middle-class family? Well, not quite. I remember going home to friends' houses after school. They'd have the television on and so I had the chance to be transported by the delights of *Blue Peter*, *Crackerjack* and *Dr Who*. Then I remember going home to my own house. We didn't have a TV but we certainly had plenty of other entertainment.

Once or twice, I walked in to find my mother posing naked in the front room while Dad painted her portrait in charcoal or oils as part of his latest course at Swansea College of Art.

'Hi there, Siân, we'll be done shortly,' called out my mum, trying not to break her pose.

'Make yourself a drink, love, and I'll get the tea on in a while,' said Dad.

It seemed the most normal thing in the world and even when I realised it was a little out of the ordinary I still loved it. Mum and Dad were true originals and full of surprises. They had the confidence to break boundaries and live their lives to the full. I was getting ready to do the same.

Chapter Two

Fashion

B right-pink pop-socks, shiny red patent leather shoes, big silver buckles, beige mini-dresses decorated with plastic diamonds... And on top of it all the favourite item in my whole wardrobe – a bright-red, wet-look PVC mac.

Pretty much my only teenage rebellions took place in the Swansea branch of Chelsea Girl. I spent every Saturday morning there with my best friend Siân Eryl. I'd save up my pocket money for weeks so I could keep on entertaining my parents with my latest look. But, while my mum would sometimes despair at my fashion taste, Dad seemed to like the fact that I wanted to stand out from the crowd. They certainly weren't going to stop me from shopping or showing off.

And it wasn't as if I was in any danger of going off the rails. I still loved school, though I think my weekly fix at Chelsea Girl was a clear reaction to the uniform. At 11, I moved to our nearest Welsh-speaking mixed secondary school, Ysgol Gyfun Ystalyfera. It was in the upper Swansea valley and the bus took about an hour to get there – plenty of opportunity to get unfinished schoolwork done.

The uniform was seriously expensive and strictly enforced. Girls wore a Welsh tapestry, blue-and-green striped pinafore dress with a turtleneck, merino-wool green sweater. We also had to wear royal-blue socks, black shoes and there was a school blazer with our coat of arms embroidered on the pocket. The only place to buy it all was at a super-posh store in Swansea called Sidney Heath. Once we got it, we had to look after it.

Lillian Powell – *Mrs* Powell to us – was one of the senior mistresses and every day she policed both our uniforms and our faces like a hawk. She would come right up to us, tilt her head and look over every inch of our faces in search of a trace of mascara or some forbidden lip-gloss. Mrs Powell also taught domestic science and she was gloriously old school with her horn-rimmed glasses and immaculate tweed jackets. I remember her spending weeks teaching us the right way to make sandwiches. 'Never salad cream, girls, always mayonnaise,' she would call out briskly. It was all a very long way from the relaxed and wonderful picnics I still had with my dad out on the Gower Peninsula.

But it wasn't as if I minded Mrs Powell's inflexibility. I didn't care what any of the teachers said. My school days began early and I loved every minute. Most mornings I was up at six, drawn out of bed by the smell of fried bacon, milky coffee and toast being made on the Aga downstairs. After eating it all up, my sister Ceri and I would walk to the local swimming baths for an hour of serious training. Having done the lengths, I'd change into my uniform at the baths before running to catch the 7.30 bus to school, my hair still half-wet and stinking of chlorine.

The training paid off. I made it into the Neath and school swimming teams and became captain of the netball team as well. Classes were just as good because I loved to learn. I was top in most subjects, took part in every theatrical production we put on, signed up to every debate and joined every choir (though I would sing softly and even mime the top notes, as I hadn't inherited my mother's beautiful voice!).

This was where my unorthodox family background really came into its own. Dad's love of debates fired us all up. By the time I attended secondary school, we were all talking about some pretty serious subjects at home. We would start off discussing books, poetry and politics but then we moved on to pollution and hot topical issues such as CND (Campaign for Nuclear Disarmament) and apartheid. We would tackle a host of broader issues as well. I remember discussions about topics such as who was responsible: the man who pulled the trigger on a gun, or the man who invented the gun? Was it the manufacturer, the designer, the individual, or someone else entirely? Maybe not the sort of thing most families spend hours talking about but the Lloyds loved it.

Dad would keep our arguments alive by playing devil's advocate – which could be infuriating and stimulating at the same time. Mum was often more emotional. She took on all sorts of left-wing causes and had long since banned South African products from the house in her stand against racial discrimination. With all this going on, it's little wonder we never really noticed that we were still one of the few families around to live without a television. With five very talkative and opinionated people sitting round the dinner table, you had to make your points fast to get them heard. Forget survival of the fittest, with us it was survival of the loudest.

Of course, this meant we saw some surprised looks on the faces of friends when they came round to dinner. Most of them couldn't believe how noisy we all were. With only two school years between Ceri and me, and three between David and me, we were a very gregarious household. Visitors often looked around for our non-existent telly and got a bit of a shock when the chess sets came out after the meal. Lots of them probably thought my bedroom was pretty weird as well. I never pinned posters of Donnie Osmond or David Cassidy on my walls. Instead, I had a pop-art print from Peter Blake and one of the wild rainbow prints by Patrick Hughes.

The great thing was that my school friends didn't care that I was different. I wasn't exactly goodie-two-shoes or a swot by doing so well in class either. My red PVC mac, illicit Mary Quant lip-gloss and all my other Chelsea Girl kit meant I was cutting edge! Dressing a la mode and being fearless helped make me popular. Yes, I was rather academic, but 'clothes shops in Swansea' would still have been my specialist subject on *Mastermind*. That's what I loved – that, and high-heeled shoes. To this day, it remains the case.

It's a bit old-fashioned but I always thought of my little group as being a bit like the 'Brodie set' from *The Prime of Miss Jean Brodie*: we were more modern, much better dressed and unlikely to go off to the Spanish Civil War to be killed. But we still had the same desire to change the world, the same belief that nothing was off limits – we couldn't have been luckier.

When my gang did start to spread its wings, we did so in suitable style. We got the train to Bath, the home of our nearest Laura Ashley store. It's hard to remember but Laura Ashley was all the rage back then – even among fashion-obsessed teenagers. Next up were weekend trips to London. Saturday lunchtime we would arrive at Paddington Station and stride on to the tube for what felt like my new spiritual home: Biba on Kensington High Street.

The loud music, the dim lights and the offbeat customers attracted me just as much as the cheap and wild fashions. Biba's founders were famous for their non-conformist, anti-establishment approach to fashion. When I read magazine articles about them, they reminded me of my parents so I wanted to be part of their world.

My love of fashion was really moving up a gear. When I'd saved up enough money, I bought suede waistcoats with long fringes. If I only had loose change, I purchased huge black-and-white plastic hoop earrings. At 14, I went through a mini-rebellion by having my ears pierced, though I kept Mrs Powell happy by sticking to gold studs when I was in class.

Back in Biba, I was also going through a Mary Quant phase and bought a wonderful black-and-white geometrical shift dress in homage to the great woman. Throw in blue-and-white spotted bell-bottoms, a long, bright canary-yellow waistcoat and a matching polka-dot cravat and I reckon I looked the business. Fortunately, I don't think I have any photographs to look at today to find out if I was right or wrong. I've got a horrible feeling I may have been wrong. Whatever, at the time I thought I was the bee's knees!

After spending hours crossing London to visit all our favourite boutiques, the girls and I would get ready for a night out. We stayed in bed and breakfasts in Sussex Gardens in Paddington. Often we got on the tube to see Shakespeare at the Roundhouse Theatre near Camden Town or went down to the National on the South Bank. In one play, we saw our hero Alan Bates naked on stage as well as lots of other plays on Shaftesbury Avenue. It wasn't exactly a wild night at the clubs but looking back I'm so proud my parents let me do all this at just 15.

I think they trusted me because we still sat down and talked around the dinner table every night. And we discussed everything, including alcohol and sex. 'I know we can trust you, Siân,' my mother would say after one of our more serious talks.

'We know you will be responsible,' said my dad.

And so I was. My parents gave me self-confidence and self-belief. Even as a child they treated me like a mini-adult and let me grow. All I needed then was to find a boyfriend – and I had one gorgeous boy in mind.

His name was Siôn and I fancied him for nearly two years. I wasn't alone. Siôn was in the year above me and he was tall with amazing hazel eyes and wavy black hair. As if that wasn't enough, he was one of the school's best rugby players. In Wales, being good at rugby beats almost everything.

FASHION

All the girls and I would literally wobble as Siôn or his mates passed us in the corridors. But for two years I thought he'd already noticed me: after all, I was always on stage collecting trophies on prize and sports days. If my parents taught me anything, it was that if you don't ask then you don't get. That's been an on-off mantra in my life. So, at 17, I decided to take matters into my own hands. I became friendly with Siôn's gang of friends and got talking to them all whenever our paths crossed. I made sure he knew there was more to me than wining awards for short stories and debating teams, that he knew I was cool. Then, after a lot of exchanged glances and flirting in the school corridors and dining hall, I moved it all up a gear. Faint-hearted feminist that I was, I plucked up the courage to ask him out.

'There's a fantastic Rodin exhibition on in London. Why don't we go?' I asked, short, direct and to the point.

Siôn looked gob-smacked by my confidence but was clearly keen. But looking at sculptures was only one part of the plan. Popping up to London was no big deal for me and I thought it was the best place to really get to know him properly.

I booked a room for the two of us in a hotel just off Russell Square in London – it was one of the places my mum used to use in town when she was there on National Union of Teachers' business so I negotiated a good deal. Back at school, everyone wanted to know exactly what we had been up to in our little London love nest but I refused to say a word. Suffice to say we had a great weekend.

From then on, Siôn and I started going steady. He would take me off on drives in his father's blue Triumph Herald.

We put Pink Floyd on the stereo and spent long, balmy and languid evenings in Mumbles or down on the Gower. They were the most sensual summers of my life. We lay on the grass in front of a barbecue and dreamed our lives away. I was still stick-thin from all that swimming and netball and I was going through a Farrah Fawcett-Majors phase in tight white jeans, pristine white tops and lashings of lip-gloss.

I'd smother myself in rich coconut oil (extraordinary to think we did that then, when nowadays I'm Ms Factor Duffle-coat when it comes to sun protection) to try to match Farrah's tan – and in the hot summer of 1976 I think I almost made it. I can't deny how good it felt to be part of a golden couple at school. I don't regret a minute of that first serious relationship. But right from the start I think we were pulling in slightly different directions.

My love of books was the most obvious. The illicit reading I'd done back home as a child had been only the start. Now I devoured books and by the time I was 16 I had finished all of D. H. Lawrence's novels, including the more obscure ones that no one else had heard of. In fact, I always maintain that I'd probably done most of my serious reading by the time I was 18 and never quite maintained that pace afterwards in my life. I was also blown away by chance phrases and striking images. L. P. Hartley's *The Go-Between* was a classic example. The first line: 'The past is a foreign country: they do things differently there' knocked me sideways. I read and re-read it. Every time I seemed to find more layers of meaning in it. It was profound and stunning and invigorating. But, when I talked to Siôn about it, I could see his brow knit together and his lovely hazel eyes become ever so slightly vacant.

FASHION

I soon realised I wouldn't get far talking about literature on our dates. Fortunately, I was happy to talk about rugby. I'm Welsh, after all. That's one of the reasons why we Welsh girls make such fantastic girlfriends.

By the time A-levels came around, I knew I'd be OK. I'd always done well at exams partly due to my good memory. It's one of the reasons why I believe that exams are no great measure of a person's intellect. So there I was, deputy head girl, the youngest-ever winner of the Crown prose prize at the Urdd National Eisteddfod, top grades at O-level under my belt and dating the most handsome boy in school. Sometimes I think I peaked at this point.

I used to head over to my grandparents' house in Maeseg to swot in peace – and to have some wonderful food. Like my dad, my grandmother was an incredible cook. Many days I sat at her kitchen table reading textbooks through the steam of a bowl of her cawl, a sort of Welsh broth full of leeks, lamb and other goodies. Her pasties were just as good. To be honest I don't think I've tasted any better to this day. As for her cakes, my grandmother was a traditional housewife who baked most mornings, which meant I always had some wonderful afternoon snacks to look forward to as well. With so much to eat, it's a wonder I got any studying done. It's also a good job I was still swimming at weekends and playing so much tennis. Otherwise, I would probably have ended up the size of a mountain.

Nowadays, food is never far from my thoughts. I can happily curl up in bed with a recipe book, devouring it in the way other people would a gripping novel. I'm always on the lookout for new recipes. If a friend tells me about a fantastic meal they've had, they'll have my undivided attention and I'll want the recipe. But the one crucial ingredient for me is great produce. I'm a big advocate of local food and like to support local farmers and growers. Cooking for friends and loved ones is a passion close to my heart, as well as my favourite way to socialise. As a child, I learned to respect food and eat a healthy diet, and I'm enormously grateful to my family for this. Bingeing on junk food and sitting on the sofa with a TV dinner is not my style!

The other reason why I liked to spend time studying at my grandparents' house was that they were pretty much the only people I knew who had as many books as we did. Their shelves were filled with a particularly eclectic mix of reading – from Marxist tracts to books of American poetry. I read my first Emily Dickinson works in front of my grandparents' fire one evening. Back then, it seemed quite normal. It's only now that I look back and think how unlikely to find such a mix of books in a former mineworker's cottage. It was an early lesson not to judge anyone by appearances or get bogged down by preconceptions.

My revision paid off and my short-term memory didn't let me down. When the A-level results came out I had a string of 'A' grades in Welsh, French and English to my name and a distinction in English at S-level. I'd also taken part of the A-level course in Latin. They were vitally important to me because I had already decided I didn't want to go to just any university. I had set my heights fairly high: I wanted to go to Cambridge.

I picked Girton College and then I wanted to do a B-Lit in Celtic Studies at Oxford. Back then, Girton was still an all-female institution. I think the faint-hearted feminist in me liked the idea of all us girls bonding – I've always been a woman's woman. I sent off my application forms. It wasn't the be-all and end-all, but with the arrogance of youth I was convinced they would welcome me with open arms. How wrong I was.

Then the letter came through. My name was typed on the front and the Girton crest – a black-and-white cross with crescents on either side – was clearly visible through the envelope. I ripped it open and sat in shock at our wonderful family kitchen. I was holding what amounted to a rejection letter. It said the board considered that despite my A-level results I was too young for the academic rigours of the college. They advised me to apply again the following year.

But I was a girl in a hurry. I was 17 and I felt ready for the world. Certainly, I couldn't see myself hanging around in Neath for 12 months while life passed me by, and in those days the gap year didn't really seem to figure. I was fired up to go to university and I wanted to go then.

'Why don't you make a late application to Cardiff?' We were all sitting round the table at dinner that night talking about my options. Mum and Dad were both clearly disappointed at my rejection but I think they liked the fact that it wasn't getting me down. So that's what I did. I rang the admissions department at Cardiff the next day. They asked for confirmation of my results and then sent an acceptance letter by return of post.

With everything set to change, the final summer in Neath seemed the perfect time for Siôn and me to consider our futures. I think we both realised our lives were heading in different directions. He too was going to Cardiff to study but we drifted apart almost the moment we arrived. Ultimately, we parted amicably and we stayed friends for many years. Looking back, I'm so proud of that. We were both still teenagers but, as break-ups go, it could hardly have been more grown up.

Packing for my big move could hardly have been more stressful, however. Apart from anything else, there were so many clothes I was desperate to take. I wanted to be me from the start and didn't want to leave anything behind. In the end, I remember squeezing my cases into Dad's car for the drive over to Llys Tal-y-Bont in Cardiff. Despite my late application, I still managed to get into a large shared flat less than a mile from the university. Better still, I was sharing with two of my old Neath pals, Suzanne and Rhian. We were all brimming with confidence and ready for anything. I waved to my mum, to Ceri and to David, as Dad revved up our blue Renault 18 for the journey. My life was about to change dramatically. Within two hours, I was going to move into my new university lodgings and within eight hours I was to meet the man who would share my life for the next 17 years.

Chapter Three
Love and Learning

His name was Mark Cavendish. Suzanne, a friend from Neath, and I met him on our first evening at the halls of residence. We were on floor C6 in a self-contained flat with five bedrooms, a kitchen and living area. Suzanne had spotted that five boys had just moved into the flat below and we wanted to check them out.

'We've just run out of coffee, let's go ask around,' was how she put it, ignoring all the brand-new coffee jars in our kitchen cupboards. So off we went.

Most people left the doors of their rooms open so it was quite easy to knock, go in and say hello. But which room to pick first? We went for Mark's because of the music he was playing. Leonard Cohen's 'Suzanne' was blaring out of his stereo and that seemed appropriate. Suzanne and I laughed as we thought of all the boys who had played that song to her back in Neath. This would give us something to talk about even if the boy playing it here didn't have much else to say.

We knocked on the door but Mark didn't hear us. We knocked again, stepped over the fat microbiology textbook holding the door open and finally attracted his attention. It was worth the extra effort. He was sitting at his desk reading a car magazine and he turned round to greet us with a big warm smile. He had really strong features and he flicked honey-blond hair away from his blue eyes to get a better look at us.

What I remember most is how relaxed and confident he seemed to be. He was wearing faded blue jeans and what looked like a hand-knitted cream-and-brown Nordic sweater. He wasn't exactly in the height of fashion but he looked comfortable in his own skin – and I like that.

As he turned the volume down on his huge stereo, Suzanne and I made our introductions. Joking about Suzanne's name and the Leonard Cohen song was a great icebreaker just as we had predicted but we soon found plenty of other things to talk about – starting with the big wooden coat of arms on the wall behind his bed. You don't see a lot of those in student bedrooms, after all.

This one had a winding figure-of-eight snake running horizontally across it and the Latin insignia *Cavendo Tutus* across the base. My A-level Latin was about to come in very useful. 'Safe by taking care, or something like that,' I said, working out the literal translation.

Mark gave me a dazzling, surprised smile. I don't think many other people had ever managed this before. 'Someone knows their Latin,' he said, with another big grin.

I could get used to those smiles, I thought. But then he

burst the bubble. I told him I was studying Welsh, English and Classical Studies Part One and he wasn't impressed – big mistake.

'Easy subject! Anyway, I thought the Welsh language was more or less dead,' he remarked. The cheek of the man! I vowed to put him straight immediately.

'Welsh is flourishing, and very much,' I laughed, after giving my language and my degree course hearty defence. Little wonder Suzanne soon steered the conversation back to calmer waters.

We then took another look at the coat of arms on Mark's wall. It turned out that *Cavendo Tutus* was his family motto. I had a vague recollection that Britain once had a Cavendish Prime Minister. I'd thought from the start that there was an air of gentility about Mark, and it turned out I was right. He also had a wonderful generosity of spirit and a great way of making people feel at home.

'Do you like chocolates?' he asked, as Suzanne and I sat on his bed.

'Who doesn't?' we replied in unison.

And he reached into the top drawer of his desk and pulled out a beautiful white box embossed with gold lettering all tied up with a pink silk ribbon. It was extraordinary. Inside were exquisite handmade chocolates he had brought back from a recent trip to Brussels. We tucked in, and we talked and talked and talked.

I was already finding something compelling about Mark. He did indeed have a very illustrious background: his father Peter was a cousin to the residing Duke of Chatsworth. Mark was clearly proud of him and I liked the way he described his ancestry and family history. He spoke of his background with ease – not talking it up but not playing it down either. He wasn't pompous; he didn't have that air of superiority we sometimes associate with the aristocracy. He didn't seem embarrassed by his privileged upbringing either.

Sitting on the edge of his bed, I wanted to know more but I tried not to interrogate him. Even today, when I meet people for the first time I always have to be careful not to fire questions at them like a machine gun. I make myself hold back, even though I'm always desperate to know more. For me, the details of people's lives are like the green vegetables of a conversation: I thrive on them. Years later my wonderful friend Stifyn Parri joked that in a ten-minute taxi journey I can find out more about the cab driver than his friends would in a lifetime. I have to admit he might be right but I think people enjoy being asked questions about themselves and even find it flattering. I genuinely want to know more about everyone I meet and I love feeling connected through the answers.

But, after about an hour or so of utterly relaxed chat with Mark, it was time for Suzanne and me to move on. There were plenty of other people in our halls of residence to meet, though I already had a suspicion that none would fascinate me as much as him.

Suzanne clearly knew how interested I was. 'So what do you think of Mr Mark Cavendish, Siân?' she asked, with a twinkle, as we headed back up to flat C6. I think that already she could tell he was more my type than hers – good news, as the last thing we either of us wanted to do was to fall for the same young man.

'He's certainly a real gentleman,' I replied, trying to stay non-committal.

LOVE AND LEARNING

Suzanne was still smiling. 'And with handmade chocolates he definitely has a taste for the finer things in life,' she said, teasing me little.

I smiled back as we climbed the stairs. It was my first day at university: I hadn't been to a single lecture or even met all my new flatmates yet but already romance seemed to be in the air.

Mark was studying microbiology and biochemistry. His laboratories were nowhere near the lecture halls and seminar rooms where I joined the other language students. And Suzanne and I really couldn't keep on going downstairs in search of coffee. I knew I had to come up with some other ideas to ensure we kept on bumping into each other. The best way was to engineer things so we both left our halls and headed for the uni at the same time. Mark had a car – a rare thing for a student back then – and he was always quick to offer a lift. The journeys didn't take long but they gave us a chance to talk one on one. By now, he really had my attention and I was hoping he felt the same.

So, as the weeks passed, I moved up a gear. I've never seen the point in waiting for something to happen if I have an instinct and it feels right.

I blagged a ticket to an evening do at the Chemistry Society that Mark had mentioned one morning in his car. I think I did pretty well in making it look as if I belonged there when he arrived. He must have taken a cue from that. From then on, he always seemed to make sure he was parked near the arts buildings at the end of lectures when I was looking for a way back to the student halls.

There was a wonderful innocence about the way we both moved our romance forward. We always acted as if we were pleasantly surprised to see each other on those 'accidental' meetings but for my part I would have been devastated if he hadn't been around as expected. It was all casual, relaxed and great fun – or at least it was until I became bed-ridden with the flu.

I'm one of those lucky people who hardly ever become ill but, when I do, I always revert to being a child. I want to be looked after, fussed over and nursed gently back to health. That's how I felt in Cardiff that autumn. Trouble was I couldn't decide who I wanted at my bedside. I started off determined to keep Mark away. After all, our romance was still at the very earliest of stages: I wasn't overly keen for him to see me coughing, spluttering, sweating and looking like death warmed up. But then I started to feel offended by his absence. Excuse me, I expected his acute concern for my health and wellbeing! So where exactly was this perfect English gentleman in my hour of need?

I told Rhian and Suzanne to sort things out and they were stars. They laid it all on with a shovel, telling Mark I was practically delirious and fading away by the minute. To his credit, he wasn't put off. Instead, he rushed to my side, ignoring the coughing, spluttering, sweating and general malaise. He made me hot drinks, mopped my brow and rose ever higher in my estimation.

I remember drifting off into a deep sleep one night after relishing his attention for an afternoon. 'I really do like Mark Cavendish,' were the last words on my mind as I closed my eyes and cuddled up with my pillow. When I woke up, I was feeling a hundred per cent better. I'm convinced the two facts are connected.

Towards the end of our first term the inevitable happened. Mark and I shared our first kiss. It wasn't in the most glamorous of locations – we were at the awful-sounding Bumpers Disco in Cardiff. But it was a magical evening. I had bounced straight back from my illness, the way I always do, so was dressed to kill and feeling fantastic.

I had arranged to meet Mark there and we didn't waste any time. The moment he saw me, he leaned over and gave me that first lingering kiss. It was totally natural and utterly wonderful. And it was romantic, even though I think the soundtrack to our kiss was some awful Seventies disco hit. From that moment on, we were a couple. Amazingly for student love affairs, we would stay together for the next 17 years.

A whole lot of factors held us together in those early days and would keep us close for so many years afterwards. I was desperate to see the world and I loved that Mark had taken a gap year before university to travel – something very few people did back then. All his stories were incredible. He had worked in a mining camp in Canada for part of his trip and fired me up with enthusiasm. We talked endlessly about different places we wanted to see. We were so young and we knew there was so much excitement ahead of us.

Living in the same building meant we could see each other pretty much all the time. We were constantly in and out of either other's little study bedroom. But we still had enough confidence to give each other plenty of space.

Mark had no problem accepting that he would always have to share my love with rugby. He loved the game and had played it at his old school, Wellington College. So many were the Saturday afternoons I would be on the touchlines when our university team was playing. And many were the Saturday nights when I would join the 'rugger buggers' at the bars to celebrate or commiserate as required. The rugby boys could set Olympic standards in the field of drinking and the amount they consumed never ceased to amaze me. It would be many years – in the bars of the House of Commons, no less – before I really saw such keen drinkers again.

But even in Cardiff I was determined not to do the boozy thing. Despite all the evenings I spent in the student bars, I don't think I had a single hangover in my entire university career. I'm not a complete goodie-two-shoes but alcohol just hits me too hard. I always wanted a clear head the next morning. I never wanted to miss anything because I was too ill to enjoy the next day. Anyway, I don't think you need to be blotto to enjoy a good night out.

When I was sipping my drinks and singing along with the rugby crowds, Mark was often at his sailing club. He trained hard and was totally committed to the sport but he never lost his sense of humour about it. I vividly remember the afternoon he burst through my door after a big race. 'Look, Siân, we won a bronze medal!' he exclaimed, happy as a small boy with a new toy.

Only a little later did he admit that the race hadn't been quite so hard fought as he had expected. Only three teams had been in it. 'We would have got the medal for just turning up,' he said and we both laughed heartily.

With a new boyfriend and a great set of friends, old and new, I have to admit that my studies took a bit of a back seat that first term at Cardiff. One of my first problems was that I missed my mum. Not in a soppy, lonely kind of way – I had always been too independent to feel like that. No, I missed Mum in a human alarm clock: 'Siân, it's time you got out of your bed and got going' kind of way.

During school time, Mum's shouts had always forced me out from under my duvet for all those 6am starts when I was a swimmer. At university, all I needed to do was to get out of bed for a few 9am lectures but without Mum's insistence even that was a bit of a problem. It took me a long time to stop turning the alarm clock off in the morning and going back to sleep. Far too many morning lectures came and went without me – or at least they did until Mark took over as my essential early-morning conscience.

The next hurdle I faced at Cardiff was the style of the work we had to do. At school, I had done well because I was given so much close guidance and so much direction. I liked structure and deadlines, and I was always quite happy being told what to do. To this day, I function best when I've got a clear brief about the job in hand. Like all my friends, I relished the sudden freedom of university life. I was in slow motion. If there didn't seem to be a particularly clear reason why I had to do a certain piece of work, then I could put it off forever. If there was no one waiting around for me to hand anything in, then it could very easily slip my mind.

The A-grade student from Ysgol Gyfun Ystalyfera was in danger of slipping behind. Luckily, I had a great little trick up my sleeve. All my life I have been fortunate enough to have some sort of photographic memory. I can look at something a few times and almost see it on demand whenever required. Today, that's pretty important because I always do the weather without an autocue – and there are a lot of facts to remember in each broadcast. As a student, it meant I could close my eyes in our exams and see large parts of essays I had written or books I had read. So I shook off all the missed morning lectures and made it through my first few terms. And by the time summer came I had plenty of other things to look forward to – Mark and I were now firmly established as a couple and I was about to meet his parents.

It could have been incredibly intimidating. Mark's family traced its history through some of England's most wonderful houses. Some of mine had passed through a string of tiny mining cottages. His father was a cousin of the Duke of Chatsworth and a NATO general in Brussels, while his mother had been to Swiss finishing schools and was a relative of the Dutch Royal Family. But I was far from being nervous. In Wales, I don't think we have the same kind of class system you get in England and elsewhere. We Welsh, on the whole, don't tend to make instant judgements based on the way people sound. We're democratic and fair, and we judge by achievements not pedigree. Even as a girl, I had been brought up to see everyone as an equal. I don't think I've ever really been intimidated by anyone in my whole life.

Fortunately, I didn't feel nervous about being on show in front of the Cavendish clan either. Like most other Welsh people, I'd been brought up to perform. From chapel to choirs to eisteddfods, we get used to being in front of people. We don't get arrogant but I think we acquire an easy confidence. That's why we perhaps make such good entertainers and such fun friends.

Of course, that doesn't mean I was totally blasé about meeting Mark's family. I was honoured he thought well enough of me to invite me home and I was curious about seeing their house and finding out about their lifestyle.

'We're the poor side of the family,' Mark had told me right from the beginning.

But this was all relative. I couldn't wait to see his eight-bedroom house on the edge of the Chatsworth Estate. In a masterstroke of understatement, the house was called Rock Cottage. Marie Antoinette could hardly have put it better.

I got the train up to Chesterfield Station and Mark met me in his grey Mini. At the house, his mother Marian welcomed me with a hug and we all headed into the kitchen for some homemade Bakewell tarts with clotted cream from the nearby Chatsworth farm. I met Mark's father, Peter, that evening at dinner. In his Harris tweeds, he looked like the ultimate country gentleman. He was just as charming as his wife was, and he mixed the strongest gin and tonics I had ever tasted.

The house itself was as beautiful as I expected. The family had some amazing paintings and tapestries on their walls but the heart of the home seemed to be in the kitchen and in the dining room – just as it was with my parents. What made the visit even more special was that the Cavendish family seemed to have just as detailed conversations around the dining table as my own. That first evening we talked about everything from population control to socialism. No wonder Mark and I seemed made for each other.

Rock Cottage and Chatsworth are within the Peak District so over the next few days Mark and I headed off on some long and wonderful walks. It was the perfect summer, made all the better because it kept springing a few extra surprises.

One of them came when I got the opportunity to meet the late Harold Macmillan. He was married to Lady Dorothy Cavendish and when I sat next to him at a formal dinner at Chatsworth House I had the chance to talk to him all evening. As I say, I don't get intimidated by people so I was able to chat to him quite easily and to all the other distinguished family members and guests around me that evening but I know it was an extraordinary experience. How many teenagers really get to talk all night with a former Prime Minister? I knew my parents and grandparents would want the fullest of reports when I got back to Wales.

Anyway, despite not having been particularly nervous, I admit that later that evening I did confess to Mark that I was relieved to have made it through the dinner without making any awful historical gaffes.

He looked up, that big smile on his face.

'Except for the champagne glass,' he said. '*What champagne glass?*'

'Harold's champagne glass.'

My mind was racing. What on earth had I done?

'You were drinking out of it all night,' eagle-eyed Mark informed me with a big smile. Poor Sir Harold hadn't been able to touch a drop and was too polite to tell me of my mistake.

Despite this incident, part of me wanted to spend the rest of the summer relaxing at Rock Cottage with Mark. Another part was ready for my next new adventure – even then I wasn't very good at sitting still.

My sister Ceri and I had long since planned a big trip across Europe. In those days, most people got inter-rail passes and travelled around by train. Ceri and I decided this was a waste of money: We were going to hitch our way through France and down into Italy. Our plan was to see the sights and meet some great people – we didn't know the half of it then.

Ceri had done most of the work mapping out our route. We planned to go through Paris and the Loire Valley before hitting the coast at Montpellier. Depending on the lifts we could get, we wanted to see the Côte d'Azur and stop in Nice, Cannes and St Tropez. Finally, we were aiming to get to Rome, Florence and as many other Italian cities as possible before heading home.

Sensible as ever, Ceri and I worked out a set of rules to make sure we stayed safe on the road. Our focus was on the hitchhiking. We would never go anywhere separately, we would only go in cars with four doors and we would always sit together on the back seat. Finally, both of us would use our individual judgement about the people who offered us rides. If either of us felt uncomfortable about someone, even if we couldn't quite put our finger on the reason why, then we would say something in Welsh to the other, wave the driver on and wait for someone else.

The strategy worked – or at least it did at first. When we got to Dover, it took less than half an hour to get our first lift into Paris. We found a cheap little hotel by the Gare St-Lazare and headed out to see the sights. That was when we made our first big mistake on the trip.

We were following in the tourist fashion of the time by carrying all our valuables in pouches around our necks. Trouble was we hadn't thought to hide these treasure troves by tucking them under our clothing. We were two teenage girls carrying our cash, passports and travellers cheques through a big crowded city – and we had it all on full display. Little wonder someone took advantage.

It happened at the base of the Eiffel Tower. It was getting dark when we got out of the Metro and gazed up at it. The whole area was buzzing with people and atmosphere. As well as all the other tourists, there were buskers, mime artists, stall holders – and robbers.

I saw the blade of a penknife pass across the front of my chest just as a hand tugged the pouch robe at the back of my neck. All my valuables were gone in what felt like the blink of an eye. And as I shouted out to Ceri I noticed the mugger was snatching her pouch in just the same way. All we had left were two ends of fraying rope around our necks.

People around us tried to help, but the robber had disappeared into the crowds. Pretty much all Ceri and I had in our pockets were the Metro tickets to take us back to our hotel. It was the first night of our adventure and it had all gone sour. How could we have been so stupid?

The following morning, we went to the Europ Assistance office in the city and to this day I thank Ceri for being sensible enough to organise policies for the pair of us. I also thank my parents for encouraging us to speak French so much at home and to study it at school. Dealing with the crisis without insurance or language skills would have been a nightmare. The first person we spoke to at the Europ Assistance desk was a lovely man called Patrick. In an immediate but indirect way, he was to change our lives.

It was clear Patrick felt sorry for us – also that in other circumstances he was the kind of person we might have as a friend. As he sorted out all the formalities of reporting the crime and replacing our possessions, we chatted. Then he asked if we were planning to stay in Paris for much longer. We smiled and said a very definite 'non'. By now, we were so tired of the city we wanted to get out fast.

He smiled back. 'I'm going to visit my best friend in the Loire Valley tomorrow morning – I can give you a lift if you want.'

It was a wonderful gesture and for Ceri, in particular, it would prove to be a life-changing event.

The three of us had a fantastic drive down south with Patrick. Already he had called ahead to Christian and his family and told them about these two Welsh girls who he felt needed some Gallic TLC. So they asked us to stay with them for a few days, extending the invitation before we had even met, which says a wonderful thing about their generosity of spirit and sense of hospitality.

When we eventually met Christian, his mother, grandmother and the rest of his family, we could see why they had acted so kindly. They were wonderful, gracious people. They were also food lovers so Ceri and I were in seventh heaven. In the course of our first fantastic meal with them in Montoire, we discovered that it was

Christian's grandmother who did most of the cooking. Over the next few weeks, we would spend many days in the kitchen with this lady. She used huge traditional copper pans and taught us some amazing new recipes, all of which we wrote down and still have today.

For nearly a week, we stayed with Christian and his family and had an incredible time. We went out on day trips visiting châteaux and exploring the local towns and villages. We bought milk from the local farm and produce from nearby markets. I soon became aware that Ceri was in no hurry to move on, too.

From that very first evening, she and Christian clicked. Within a matter of days, they were holding hands and all but professing undying love for each other. It was lovely to witness but I took a while to get used to it. I was Ceri's big sister and we were a long way from home so I had to be protective of her. But then I looked at Christian and his family and started to relax. There seemed to be something inevitable about the romance. They were perfect for each other from the start – the ultimate proof that you really can fall in love at first sight. All these years on, they are happily married and living in Paris.

But back on our trip I had itchy feet. Ceri and I had planned to head all the way down to Rome and I wanted to get back on the road. We agreed to come back through the Loire on our return so the lovebirds could meet again. Then Ceri and I packed our rucksacks and Christian dropped us off on the main road which would take us south.

'That was absolutely wonderful. Can you believe how well that turned out? We'll never get as good a lift as that again,' I said, as we stuck out our thumbs. But we did – and almost straight away. Our European adventure was about to get even better too.

Just outside Rome, an Italian man in a big red Range Rover stopped for us. He was in his forties and introduced himself very formally as Roberto Benelli. I instinctively trusted and liked him. He was dressed smartly in a white shirt, beige trousers and, as we saw when he got out to help with our bags, shiny new Italian loafers. He smelled of expensive aftershave, spoke great English and was the perfect gentleman. This time around, there would be no love interest, not least because Ceri was already pining for Christian and I was dreaming of Mark, but both of us felt instinctively that Roberto could become a firm friend.

It turned out that he felt the same.

As we raced down towards Florence, we learned that he had recently come out of a painful divorce and was lonely. He asked if we wanted to stay at his house just outside of the city – making it quite clear that we would have our own rooms and be totally safe. Hopefully, Ceri and I are both good judges of character. We felt we could trust this man and we knew we could look after ourselves. Plus we wanted a good base from which to explore Florence. The more we saved on hotel bills, the more we could spend on museum entries and other attractions. We said we would love to stay.

What a house it turned out to be. It had what seemed like dozens of bedrooms and was fully staffed with a small army of butlers, maids and cooks. In the garage, Roberto had a collection of some 40 cars – everything from classic Minis to Ferraris. The chemical company his family owned was clearly doing pretty well. I joked with Ceri that I should perhaps have picked a science degree rather than sticking to the arts.

After being shown our rooms – which were like something out of a Merchant Ivory film – Ceri and I headed out to see the sights of Florence. We went to the Uffizi Gallery, we walked over the Ponte Vecchio and we had a hot and aimless day wandering around the Boboli Gardens. Whenever we got back to base, there were more surprises in store. Our conversations in the car had told Roberto that we were both confirmed food fanatics, so he had decided to take us to a series of Italy's best restaurants – by helicopter.

It was the first time either of us had travelled like that but what a way to see the Italian countryside. We passed over the rolling hills with those classic cypress trees and ancient farmhouses on our way to yet another incredible meal. We wandered along the waterside after eating on the isle of Elba, we flew for meals at Roberto's hunting lodge in the Tuscan hills, and we sat at candlelit tables gazing down at the landscape below the wonderful Fiesole opposite Florence.

It was a glorious, innocent time and I remember thinking how right it had been for us to step out of our comfort zones and go hitching in the first place. Roberto was passionate about his helicopter. He would do stomach-churning and heart-stopping 'tricks' with steep dives and sudden swerves when Ceri and I least expected it. 'We're using a gallon of fuel a minute,' he would boast. That wouldn't have gone down so well with the Siân of modern times! At the time, there seemed to be nothing wrong with that, but in our defence we didn't know that then.

LOVE AND LEARNING

Ceri and I stayed with Roberto for nearly a week. He was clearly lonely and enjoyed having two enthusiastic young girls to impress and show around. We genuinely took pleasure in his company. It was innocent and lovely. Not once did he make any sort of pass at either of us. We never once felt we were taking advantage of his hospitality or outstaying our welcome. Indeed, when we finally did decide to move on, Roberto seemed desperately sad to be left on his own again.

This charming man kissed our hands when we said our goodbyes at the motorway. I remember saying in one of my letters back to Mark what an old-fashioned and wonderfully Italian gesture it was, which made us feel everything in the world was good and decent.

The experience also convinced Ceri and me that no one would ever have better hitchhiking stories than we had. As it turned out, Mark's brother Simon certainly came close. When he had been in Central America, he got a lift from a friendly older man in a battered old Range Rover. They had driven slowly through the countryside, making regular stops because the driver, a man called Richard, wanted to chat to some of the men working in the sugar-beet fields. After a wonderful day, Simon asked for the man's address so he could write and thank him for his kindness. He had a fantastic response.

'Just address the envelope to Richard Tate, Belize. It will get to me.'

He had been given a tour of the sugar fields by Mr Tate from Tate & Lyle!

Back in Italy, Ceri and I were convinced that no ride could ever be better than Mr Benelli. Our robbery in Paris had also become just a fading memory. Little wonder we let our guard down – it was a mistake.

After a few more safe and uneventful rides, we were back in northern Italy and hoping to return to Christian in the Loire Valley but after three hours in the hot sun we started to feel desperate. No one would stop for us so we broke one of our cardinal rules: we agreed to climb into a tiny two-door car.

It was a brown Fiat and it was dirty, smelled of oil and just didn't feel right. We also didn't like the look of our driver. Like Roberto, most Italian men were immaculately dressed and turned out – Ceri and I both loved that. This man wasn't. He was in his fifties, had thinning hair and was wearing grubby jeans and an un-ironed shirt. Something about the way he looked at us set warning bells off in my mind right from the start but I tried to ignore them as our driver slammed the door shut and pulled out into the traffic.

We had been on the road for about 20 minutes before I saw it. We had just pulled into the fast lane and I glanced at our driver to check he was paying enough attention to the road. Instead, he seemed far more interested in looking at us in his rear-view mirror. That's when I noticed he had taken his right hand off the steering wheel. You can probably guess where it was heading.

Ceri had seen it as well: '*Mae'r dyn hwn ar fin dechrau chwarae gyda'i hunan tra'n gyrru.*' Which roughly translates as: 'I think he's going to start playing with himself while he's driving.'

She was right. Our driver pulled down the zip on his jeans and got going. Ceri screamed for him to stop and let us out. But he ignored us and we were still in the fast lane of an Italian motorway. I wasn't scared of what this sad little man was doing but I was afraid of what it might be leading up to and so I tried desperately to calm my sister down.

'Ceri, we're in the middle of traffic – he can't just let us out. Stay calm, this will pass: it's going to be all right,' I told her, trying to persuade myself just as much as her.

Meanwhile, our driver had something to say as well.

'*Scusa, scusa, scusa* – I couldn't help myself,' he said, taking his eyes off the road yet again and looking at both of us through the mirror. He was clearly ashamed of what he was doing, but not so concerned that he would stop until his dirty little job was done.

When it was over, he stopped the car in a lay-by. Ceri and I grabbed our bags and climbed over the front seat and out of his car fast.

'Excuse, excuse, excuse,' he repeated before zooming off.

It's hard to see just how he could have got any pleasure from what he'd just done but he certainly put Ceri and me on our guard again for the rest of the trip.

Back at Christian's country home in the Loire Valley, it was clear that I was now a gooseberry. For Ceri, this was far more than a holiday romance: she and Christian have now been married for over 20 years and live happily in the heart of Paris. And all because we were so desperate to leave the city after being robbed. It just goes to show how black clouds really can have silver linings.

Chapter Four

The Good Life

Luckily for me, I too had a wonderful relationship to return to after our road trip across Europe. In our second year at Cardiff, Mark and I moved into a big Victorian house on Colum Road with a group of friends. We were a mixed bunch – Max and Chris Roberts, who along with his wife Sally remain good friends to this day, were studying accountancy; Mark Olliot was reading economics; Claire Cleverdon and Debbie More did history and Ross Owen read archaeology.

But opposites clearly attract for none of us stopped talking and 6 Colum Road was to host some of the best parties of the year. We also served some of the finest home-cooked food. Not for us a life lived on traditional student fare like chips, Chinese takeaways and kebabs, we were more *The Good Life* than *The Young Ones*. We baked our own bread, we grew herbs and vegetables in our little garden and even made our own yoghurt. Add in the home brew that the boys created in our airing cupboard and we were pretty much self-sufficient. Every supermarket and off-licence in Cardiff could have closed down and I reckon our house would still have put on a decent party.

As if we weren't close enough at home, the gang all got part-time jobs together as well. We worked at the Sherman Theatre just around the corner. As well as giving us some extra cash, it meant we could go in and see films for free whenever we wanted. I remember seeing *Annie Hall*, *Blade Runner* and a real mix of blockbusters and art-house films. I also recall feeling a bit tense after seeing *The Big Chill*. Its storyline of a group of thirty-something graduates having a tense reunion after one of their number commits suicide seemed a little too close for comfort. I didn't want to think that our charmed lives might ever end.

The other great thing about living in Colum Road was its location. It was right next to the university so I could stay in bed even later in the morning and still get to my early lectures. Well, at least that was the theory. In reality, I think my bed was so comfortable I still missed far too many.

Living with Mark was as good as I hoped – we talked all the time and seemed to share more and more interests. I was thrilled when I realised he loved scouring the second-hand bookshops of Hay-on-Wye as much as I did. For me, it was like those days in the Ty John Penry Welsh bookshop in Swansea with the postal orders I won in my short-story competitions. Bookshops are treasure troves to me and it was wonderful Mark felt the same – though that didn't stop me taking the mickey out of all the trashy science fiction he would buy.

So was everything in our relationship absolutely rosy? It was – until the next summer Mark started to teach me to drive. I'd had a provisional licence since the age of 17. It's a cliché that driving lessons can destroy even the strongest of relationships. Mark and I nearly proved that like all clichés it is founded in truth.

Our one and only session took place in the fields near Rock Cottage in Derbyshire. Far from the nearest road, we didn't think anything could go wrong. And as I'd had a couple of BSM lessons already I was convinced I didn't need to pay much attention to Mark's instructions. Like I say, I pick up information fast. What else did I have to know? Anyway, I climbed over into the driving seat as Mark walked around to open the passenger door. I turned the ignition on – and stalled. I tried again, headed across the field, failed to get into second gear and stalled. I tried again, made it into second and then went back to first because for some reason I couldn't find third – I stalled.

Nothing unusual in any of this and not so bad, really, for a first attempt in a new car. But like a sitcom couple Mark and I started to get increasingly irritated with each other. He kept saying I wasn't paying attention to his instructions, I said he was patronising me. And when he mentioned his mother, well, I over-reacted, like a sitcom wife.

'You know my mother warned me about teaching you. She said it never works when you try to teach your partner and she was right,' Mark exploded.

I snapped. 'Fine,' I said, turning off the engine. 'It's over.'

'So, will you go back to BSM?'

'No, Mark, it's over between us. I'm not going to be spoken to like that. Now that I've seen what you're really like I'm going back to Rock Cottage. I'm going to pack my bags and I'm going to go home.'

I stormed out of the car, slammed the door and marched across the field to the house. Who knew I had such depths as a drama queen? Fortunately for everyone, Mark was ready to put his diva in her place. He ran after me, kissed me and said how sorry he was. That autumn I signed up with BSM again and passed my test second time around. Today even Mark will agree I'm a decent driver.

Having survived our one and only fall-out in the fields near Rock Cottage, Mark and I were ready to get even closer. Back in Cardiff, we didn't fancy another shared student house: we wanted a place of our own. I hadn't even turned 20 and I was settling down. No wonder I'm having so much fun in life today. I got the whole middle-aged thing out of my system in my twenties.

We rented a tiny attic flat in the eaves of a big townhouse on Severn Grove in Cardiff's Canton district. It was owned by one of the university psychology lecturers and we shared a bathroom with some post-grad students downstairs. And when I say 'tiny', I mean *tiny*. A thin hardboard wall divided up one ordinary-sized room into two so we had a minute bedroom and an equally small living room. Our kitchen was the size of a sofa and the only space for the fridge was next to our bed but I think it was the happiest home in Cardiff.

Mark and I spent hours in charity shops and car boot sales to furnish our little space. His family might be aristocracy but he was expected to make his own way in life. He certainly didn't have some big trust fund income to spend and I don't think I would have liked it if he had. Hunting for bargains and saving up for special items made even the most ordinary items more valuable to us. Today I've still got some pictures from Severn Grove on my walls in mid-Wales. Just looking at them reminds me of an endless number of good times.

We were having dinner in our living room one night when Mark told me he wanted to give up on his degree. After failing one set of exams and re-sits, he had already been held back a year and he couldn't see things getting better.

'It's going nowhere for me,' he said. 'It's not just that I'm doing badly, it's that I'm not enjoying it any more.'

I wasn't going to argue with him. I think you need passion to make the most out of a degree course; it's so much easier if you're fired up with a desire to learn. If not, its just boring.

Within a week, Mark quit his course and I admired him for making his decision and acting upon it so fast. What he did next was a surprise, though: he got a job in the cold storage unit of a meat warehouse on the outskirts of the city. This was a man whose great-great-grandfather had been Prime Minister. Now he was earning next to nothing lugging frozen carcasses around alongside some of the toughest workers in our city. A lot of girlfriends might have been appalled, but I thought it was interesting. It proved just how open Mark was; it showed he didn't judge anyone or anything. Just like my parents, he was prepared to defy convention and live his own life his own way. I loved it and tried to learn from it.

I also loved the fact that Mark brought some great cuts

of lamb home with him at the end of his shifts. He might not have been earning much but we never ate better. When my final exams approached, I used to joke that I might soon need a job right alongside my boyfriend. Missing all those morning lectures no longer seemed quite so funny. I had to catch up fast and my semi-photographic memory was to be put to its biggest test to date.

Some good friends on the course lent me their notes as I struggled to catch up with what I had missed. I amazed myself by being able to get up at 4am to go through the books I should have read months earlier. And I looked over all the past examination papers to try to work out what sort of questions were likely to come up. What helped enormously was my ability to get straight to the heart of a subject. I am blessed with an ability to skim through any amount of information fast and pick out all the salient points. Then I can remember it and repeat it as required. But would this do the trick?

I walked into my finals with everyone else and crossed my fingers as we waited to see the questions. I got lucky – several of the topics I expected to appear were on the papers and I could close my eyes and see most of the information I needed to answer them. As I walked out of the examination hall, I was pretty sure I had passed but when the results were announced I got the shock of my life.

My professor broke the news to me over the phone. 'Well, Siân, you've done quite well. You've got a first,' he announced.

I was euphoric! *Quite* well! That was the understatement of the year.

I sobered up a bit. This was incredible news. I knew my

parents would be absolutely thrilled. And there was still more to come.

'Actually, you've got the highest mark in the university. Well done, Siân,' he concluded, saving the very best for last.

I was shaking as I hung up, dialled my parents' number and then called Mark. To this day, I still can't quite believe I did so well. I have often wondered what exactly the criteria could have been when I was being compared to so many other students in so many different disciplines but the award was genuine. I was given hundreds of pounds' worth of book tokens – all my life I seem to have been winning book tokens. Then I was told I had the honour of reading the proclamation – in Latin – at the Honorary Degree Ceremony of the University of Wales in Cardiff that summer.

'Oh, and one more thing,' the ceremony organiser told me, almost as an afterthought as he explained my role, 'Prince Charles will be in the audience so we need everything to go particularly well.' No pressure there then.

Fortunately, I had ample confidence from my A-level Latin and from all the other public performances I had given since childhood. The ceremony took place in Cardiff University's Great Hall, a room packed with the great, the good, the academic and the artistic. When my moment arrived, I found myself wondering how many people in this vast room would understand a word of what I was saying. Very few, I concluded to myself.

There was a big reception afterwards and I mingled happily with some of the university's top brass and our most illustrious guests. As usual, I wasn't scared or intimidated by anyone. People are people is how I see it –

they're either interesting and polite or they're not, but you won't find out if you don't strike up a conversation.

That attitude allowed me to approach the artist Graham Sutherland. I loved his tapestry *Christ in Glory* that hung in Coventry Cathedral and the prints he had created for the Shell Oil Company. I was also aware of his lifelong love of West Wales and was a big fan of the works of art he'd undertaken down in Pembrokeshire. The chance to talk to one of my favourite living artists was too good to miss. And it turned out Graham was just as welcoming and fascinating as I had hoped. We talked for nearly an hour in the mêlée of the post-ceremony reception. I asked about his work and he told me more about the whole creative process behind it. We talked about his days in Menton in the South of France and his gallery in Picton Castle in West Wales. As we said our goodbyes, he invited me to tea, but sadly he was to die before I had the chance to enjoy his hospitality. To this day, I have a vivid memory of his piercing baby-blue eyes. And the love of my life, Jonathan, has those exact same eyes.

I did speak to one other man at that ceremony who I would meet many more times in the years ahead – Prince Charles. Still in my gown and mortar, I was walking towards one of the exits, when the Prince was heading for one of the others. Apparently, he recognised me as the Latin-speaking prizewinner so he changed direction to come and congratulate me.

'Well done on the Latin!' he said, as his bodyguards milled around.

I thanked him and smiled, and that was it. So many

years later, it's wonderful to think I've been to Highgrove and St James's Palace and I've helped with promotional films for the Prince's Trust. Our connection began with a few lines of Latin at a graduation ceremony.

The only bad news that summer was that Mark and I had to start buying our own lamb cuts again. He had moved on from the meat warehouse and started a new job in the computer industry – where he still works today. My own next move was to take me out of Cardiff, though Mark and I knew our relationship was strong enough to cope. I had won a scholarship to do a B-Lit in Celtic Studies at Jesus College, Oxford. It was time to say goodbye to Wales, though this turned out to be easier said than done.

I loved the dreaming, gleaming spires of Oxford but I think I knew from the very first moment that I didn't fit in academically among the post-grads. At 21, I was at the university at research level – and that was very different from the undergraduate world. I was surrounded by the best of the best: people focused entirely upon knowledge and science and the arts and academia. They had the most impressive brains; one day they might change the world but, as the old cliché goes, one or two of them couldn't boil an egg in the meantime. Nor could others give two hoots what they looked like or how they dressed or anything else.

I'm embarrassed to admit that all this intensity and excellence didn't exactly bring out the best in me. My dad had always shown me how to play devil's advocate in an argument. Now I seemed to be taking on the role in real life. It meant that the more serious my colleagues became, the frothier and more frivolous I felt. I started to dress in an even more trendy style and attended precious few lectures – I found some wild and wonderful things in the town's charity shops. My heels became even higher and I clicked and clattered my way through those marbled halls. I loved the parties and the restaurants and socialised to my heart's content. I felt a bit of a cheat, to be honest.

I've always had a keen sense for the theatre of the absurd. This was Samuel Beckett and Jean Genet and Harold Pinter writ large. And I was well aware that suddenly I was a mass of contradictions. Back in Cardiff, I had been happy to settle down with Mark like some kind of middle-aged, married couple; at home, I always thrived on intense political and intellectual debates. Now I was on my own in Oxford I wanted to trip the light fantastic and show people how to get a life.

I don't think there was ever any real chance that I would last out my full course, but I didn't even give it my best shot. Every Sunday night or Monday morning after a weekend back in Cardiff with Mark, I would be back on the National Express coach to Oxford to try to knuckle down. I remember having Fleetwood Mac's *Rumours* playing on my personal stereo for those long boring rides. It was the new soundtrack of that part of my life.

One thing I didn't worry about in my Oxford days was Mark's fidelity. It wasn't even something we felt the need to discuss. We both instinctively felt that neither of us would cheat. I knew he was honourable and honest, and, had I wanted to stay at Oxford to complete my degree, I knew Mark would have supported me in every way possible. But it never came to that.

THE GOOD LIFE

Halfway through my first year, I decided it was time to quit. I felt bad giving up such a prestigious scholarship. I felt sorry for my parents – especially as my sister Ceri had almost simultaneously given up her degree in Edinburgh to go and live in France with Christian – but it was exactly what I needed to do. At this time, though, David was on his way to university in Manchester, so Mum and Dad still had one child in education!

It also turned out that my timing was spot-on. A part-commercial, part-community radio station was about to go on air in Cardiff. It was run by someone I had admired for years and I was determined to get a job in his team. Almost on a whim and totally out of nowhere, I was about to become a broadcaster.

Chapter Five

Radio Days

I decided I might as well be myself in my job interview. Back then I was not the kind of person to wear a safe black trouser suit so I wore a lime-green cashmere sweater from a charity shop, bleached white drainpipes and purple trainers covered in glitter. Oh, and I had just had my hair cut fairly short and had spiked it up with gel. They might not give me the job, I thought, but at least they'll see the real me.

While I had been at Oxford, my old Colum Road friend Chris Roberts had told me that the radio star Dan Damon had been made programme controller of a new Welsh-speaking radio station to be called the Cardiff Broadcasting Company (CBC). I had been a fan of Dan's for ages – he was a great presenter and years ago I had loved listening to him learn Welsh live on air on Radio Wales. I'd never even considered working for a radio station before but I did like the idea of working with Dan. And the new station would give me the chance to use my Welsh. With absolutely no journalistic training or radio experience, I decided to go for it.

Looking back, it was a bit like asking Siôn out on a date back at school. Back then I'd felt that, if you don't ask, you don't get. It worked out then and it has worked out ever since for me. I've never had a problem being open to all sorts of things. I don't mind the possibility of rejection – all I care about is the thought of being an old woman who regrets all the things she was too scared to try.

So I wrote in to Dan Damon. He asked me in for a chat. And he seemed to like me – coloured clothes, sparkly shoes, crazy hair and all. Of all things, we started off talking about the weather. Then he got down to business.

'So, are you really bilingual or just good at Welsh?' he asked.

'Bilingual,' I said firmly.

'The Breakfast Show goes on air at six so you will need to be in at five. Do you think you can do that?'

'Yes, I can.'

'Every day?'

'Yes.'

'And we can only pay you £20 a week. But if you stick at it you'll earn more.'

'Yes, that's fine.'

He explained more about my role, more about the station and its aims. We were trying to drink cups of coffee as the studio was set up around us. Desks were being moved in, computer screens and equipment connected on all sides. It seemed incredibly exciting. So, while the early mornings petrified me and the salary was little more than pocket money, I was desperate to get going. I had this underlying worry that I had let people down by dropping out of Oxford. Using my language skills and carving out a high-profile career like this would prove I hadn't made a mistake. I wanted to show that I could make it in the real world.

CBC turned out to be the ultimate baptism of fire. We only had time for a few early-morning dry runs before we went live, but we were a close-knit gang, all in it together. A number of my colleagues from those early days have carved flourishing broadcasting careers for themselves – Martyn Shakleman on BBC national radio, Vaughn Roderick as the political supremo at BBC Wales and Eifion Jones on Radio Cymru and Channel 4 Wales, S4C.

I started my days in darkness. I soon found out that I needed to be in at 4.30, not five, as Dan had promised. As I rushed through the empty streets, I felt like the only person in the city. However quiet it was, my adrenaline was already flowing. The looming deadlines meant I had to hit the ground running the moment I got to the studio. On arrival, my first task was to go through the news feeds from Independent Local Radio. These listed all the overnight events, ongoing stories and diary items for the day ahead. I had an hour to sift through for the ones I thought would mean the most to our audience. Anything with a Cardiff angle got priority, though I was able to use my own judgement and pick whatever I thought would work.

Then I had to translate the information into Welsh, which took a little longer than I had expected. Because it was going out on radio this wasn't just a case of changing stories word for word. They had to be rewritten as well so they flowed in the new language. And the clock was always ticking, the pressure always on.

When the first batch of news was done, I had to move on to the travel information. We used a local cab company – Metro – to let us know what was happening in the heart of Cardiff, then I called the AA for a broader picture of the area. I then rang British Rail to check on any train delays or crashes. I had to write it all up, timed to fit our travel slot, before our first bulletin that went out live just after six.

I sat at the desk in studio one waiting for the red light to go on. Then I leaned in to the big black overhanging microphone and had my big moment.

'*Bore Da*. Good morning. This is Siân Lloyd with the news headlines.'

The moment I went off air I was back at the news feeds to update the early-morning stories. At this point, I started to chase the Welsh angle even harder. If there was a national story about hospital waiting lists, then I would get on the phone to as many Welsh hospitals as possible; I marshalled together the facts and figures and arranged interviews with their spokespeople. On Budget Day I would have typical Welsh families lined up to talk about their finances and on the first day of the school terms I was ready with teachers and headmasters and even nervous children. Every day was different and you couldn't relax for a second.

At 6.30, I was back on air again, reading my updated stories. Ten minutes later, I was back on to my travel contacts to give the next set of traffic alerts – I even did the weather! It was fast and furious stuff, and it was an incredible break for someone with no journalistic training – and someone with a lifelong hatred of early starts. To this day I'm so grateful to Dan for seeing something in me that he could trust. It was partly my enthusiasm, partly my ability to take a brief fast and get on with the job with a minimum of fuss, but really I know he was taking a gamble on me. I was determined not to let him down.

Mum and Dad were thrilled for me. Mum couldn't believe that I made it to my desk so long before dawn each day. She laughed when she heard my early-morning routine. I had five alarm clocks all timed to go off at exactly one minute apart. And I had Mark. He had woken me early to help me cram for my exams at Cardiff. Now he made me strong coffee even earlier each morning as my five-minute pre-dawn chorus went off. Hero that he is, he even drove me into the studio.

Mark had remained in our attic flat while I had been in Oxford and it had been great to move back in with him. But domestic life wasn't exactly easy when my contribution to our weekly budget was just £20. I think the Saturday girls in my beloved Chelsea Girl were probably making more than that back then.

Fortunately, Dad had taught me to think on my feet in the kitchen. I'd stretch our shopping money to the limit. Chinese Pork belly with tinned pineapple, anyone? What about stuffed hearts? Or pretty much any soup that could be conjured up in our new Moulinex blender. I reckon I turned very little into some great soups, purées and mousses. Some nights I even became a proper little Stepford Wife. I would cook and entertain Mark's computer bosses in our tiny little living room. Strangely enough, we suited being Terry and June for a while, though with our ridiculously early starts our dinner parties didn't ever run on that late.

Despite those early starts and the cracking pace, I thrived on life at CBC. I felt at home there and knew I had been right to leave Oxford. The only downside was that our staff turnover was incredibly high. We were a fledgling station and built around a complicated half-commercial, half-community structure. It meant funding was precarious and good people let go at an alarming rate. Very often I would say goodbye to colleagues at the end of a shift and come back the next day to find they had gone. 'See you tomorrow' was a risky phrase to use back then. Forget a job for life, we couldn't rely on one for more than a day.

In all the ups and downs I've experienced during my broadcasting career, ITN colleagues have often said how relaxed I seem to be about cost-cutting and redundancy programmes. I say it's because I saw the brutal nature of the media so early in my career: I learned how fragile our employment could be.

I never had that obsessive desire to get into broadcasting. In 1979, I just wanted to use my Welsh and to work with a man I had admired since I was a little girl. Apart from that, I simply wanted to enjoy the ride as long as it lasted.

Today, people ask me the secret to being the longest-standing female weather forecaster in the country. If I can answer that at all, I think it's because I've never had some complicated, long-term game plan. Instead, I just wanted to enjoy whatever came my way and I accepted that it could all end at any time. I think my biggest career weakness, but also my greatest strength, has been a lack of steely ambition.

So in the bad times at CBC I was happy to pitch in and do a variety of tasks. I translated the news headlines and presented an absurdly late evening show; I always tidied the studio at the end of my shift and made coffee for everyone. And over time I saw my on-air role get bigger and broader. Ironically enough an early promotion was to read out the weather as well as the news and traffic reports.

But I also went out into the field to do vox pops on local or national issues. The engineering department gave me one of the little Marantz portable tape recorders used by radio journalists at the time, and I hit the streets to speak to passers-by. And my remit included some tough subjects. One of the first roving reports I did was on female genital mutilation. I researched and recorded reports on gay adoption, gypsy camps and just about anything else required of me. Can you imagine the average commercial station going anywhere near those topics nowadays?

We also handled breaking news and I learned how important it was to stay professional and keep your voice steady, however bad you felt inside. Though it might seem comparatively lightweight today, my first test came when we got the news that John Lennon had been shot in New York. All I could think as I got the story ready was that my dad had loved John so much and that my mum had written out some of his lyrics to teach them to the kids at school as poetry.

A FUNNY KIND OF LOVE

Our CBC breakfast show ended sharply at nine. Whoever was still employed on the morning team would then head off to a greasy spoon round the corner for bacon sandwiches and omelettes. We would hold post-mortems into the day's show and start planning for the next day. It felt good to watch some of the other bleary-eyed people come into the café and to know they still had a full day's work ahead of them. But it didn't feel good enough to really compensate for my five alarm calls at 3.30am each morning.

With the endless hiring and firing going on around me at CBC I was thrilled to have lasted a full year. I had also made plenty of good friends. Things were about to get even better. As I passed my first anniversary, still only earning a little more than the paltry £20-a-week starting wage, Dan suggested I go to London for some more formal training.

The station paid my fees at the National Broadcasting School, which was on Greek Street in Soho. The iconic Gay Hussar restaurant was practically next door and I desperately wanted to save up enough to eat there. The restaurant was famous for its links to politics, journalism, the arts and debate. Labour party members had made it an institution. It was the kind of place some of my family would have loved; people like Michael Foot used to go, so you can imagine the kind of conversations they could have had!

Keith Belcher and John Wellington were among my early instructors at the NBS and I was determined to be a perfect pupil. I thrived on getting some proper training at last. For the past year, I had been working on the hoof every day, just doing whatever it took to produce the best broadcasts. Learning some of the theory and putting everything in context was brilliant. And the more I learned about slander, libel and all the other pitfalls radio presenters could face, the more grateful I was that I'd not slipped up so far.

I also fell in love with the look and feel and excitement of London itself.

I slept at the women's youth hostel near Tottenham Court Road for my first few nights then I moved to a shared flat up in Highgate, North London. I had my first visit to the House of Commons as part of the political news classes and did some court reporting at the Old Bailey, and I adored being part of the Soho set. My classmates and I would start our evenings hanging out in one of the coffee shops on Old Compton Street. Then because we would talk to anyone around us we would often get invited to dinners, clubs, pubs and parties. It was a great time. We all had so little money but we somehow had so much fun.

We went to the theatre all the time – we were always at concerts or other events. Looking back, I just can't work out how we managed to afford it all. I think we just blagged our way into some places, begged discounts at others and somehow made it all work. I could have lived that life for years. But the course only lasted a matter of months and all along I knew my heart – and, of course, Mark – were back in Wales.

Soon I was back on the M4 on another National Express coach hoping my new broadcasting qualifications would win me some even bigger challenges. I was happy to be going back to CBC but I also kept my eye out for other opportunities. All my life I've liked being stretched academically and professionally; I don't like stagnating. So when I saw one particular job advert in the media section of the Monday *Guardian* I thought I had found my perfect new role.

BBC Wales was looking for a researcher for its evening magazine show, *Wales Today*. In some ways, this could have been a step down for someone who had been writing and presenting her own stuff on CBC but we were still just a strange, hybrid little station. BBC Wales was the mainstream. I might be small fish there but it would be a much bigger pond. And once more I don't think going for this new job was anything to do with ambition for its own sake. I just felt I wanted to prove myself again; I needed to get out of my latest comfort zone and test myself.

Trouble was, I knew I wouldn't be alone in applying. Even then, in the early 1980s, *Guardian* adverts attracted scores if not hundreds of replies. Competition would be tough, but then that was just how I liked it. My CBC experience and my NBS course got me an interview and an hour-long general knowledge test. What does OPEC do? What did BOC stand for? Who is Boutros Boutros-Ghali? I must have got enough of them right because I got the job.

Being a researcher suited me. I can speed-read a lot of information and spot what matters. The schoolgirl whose précis work was always read out to class as an example was in her element at the BBC. The main editor on *Wales*

Today was David Morris Jones. Everyone said DMJ had a weird take on life but from day one I responded well to it.

I loved his offbeat story ideas. They reflected my sense of the surreal and the absurd. When the massive snowfalls came to Cardiff on 7–8 January 1982, there was an outcry over the people charging extra for shovels and essentials like bread and milk. But instead of following up on the anger DMJ wanted to turn the story on its head. Despite our hearty disapproval, he did a slot on the snow entrepreneurs!

Because he and I sometimes thought in the same quirky way, I got to develop my role faster than might have been expected. I started out assisting reporters with the logistics; I helped book the crews for jobs and to check everyone was able to get from A to B in time. This gave me an incredibly good grounding into the nitty-gritty of television. It meant I never took anything for granted when I finally got onscreen myself – I knew how much work had always been done behind the scenes.

On *Wales Today*, I soon went from pure research into a minor reporting role. I helped out some of my senior colleagues and even did some interviews when no one else was available. My face never made it onscreen, but my voice made it on to the air. It was a start.

Getting a mainstream job at the BBC offered two more benefits. One was security – it was a world away from the chaos of CBC. It also looked great on my CV. But after a year I was ready to move on and I admit I took my next job for the strangest of reasons. If I'd had that forensic career plan that I saw in so many of my broadcasting colleagues, I would have climbed up the greasy pole in

Cardiff and then applied for every job going in London. Instead, I got it into my head that I wanted to work for a quango in the middle of nowhere.

I could still be a girly city girl who loved clothes and shoes and make-up, and knew every boutique, high-street store and charity shop like the back of her hand, but I seemed to have a bizarre puritanical streak in me as well. So one morning I just woke up and decided it would be wrong for me to spend my whole life in towns and cities. I felt as if being in the countryside would be good for my soul. It turned out I was right, but I still have no idea where these sudden thoughts really come from.

The job advert was in the good old *Western Mail*, the national daily newspaper. The Development Board for Rural Wales was looking for a press officer and, because of the rural nature of the job, it had to be someone who could drive. The idea was to make sure that businesses, tourists and the world in general got to know more about rural mid-Wales. So many other parts of the principality were booming and it didn't seem right that such a big area was missing out. The old puritanical streak in me was convinced I was tailor-made to turn all this around. Unbelievably, I didn't even have a full driving licence. I must have misled them into thinking that I could already drive but I actually passed my test in Cardiff just a week before embarking on my new job and life in rural mid-Wales. Talk about tempting fate!

When I got the post at the age of 24 and started work, I can't pretend I became terribly worthy. Hair shirts were never my thing. I wanted to have fun and I got my way. The team and I had an absolute ball getting the mid-Wales message out there. We hosted fashion shows on the Orient Express; we took local mid-Wales food and other produce to fairs and festivals around the country; we organised concerts and parties and awards ceremonies... I was constantly on the phone or meeting high-profile people, from business leaders to arts company bosses. Almost always I was the youngest person at most of our big meetings and presentations but I never felt out of my depth. Never exactly lacking in confidence, I gained even more as I did whatever it took to promote my new region. I believed passionately in my cause and I loved the challenge of getting that message across.

Home life was just as good. Mark had moved out to the country with me. We got a flat in Newtown, where strangely enough the local MP would one day be a certain Mr Lembit Opik. Long before that nightmare, Mark and I were still a dream couple. He had an open-topped MG Midget, and Bruce Springsteen became the latest soundtrack to our lives as we raced around making lifelong friends.

Newtown is an ancient market town in a bend of the River Severn. It had some beautiful old buildings at its heart and stunning countryside just outside. Social reformers such as the Co-Op founder and trade unionist Robert Owen were born there, so it had the right campaigning vibe for me. Today it has food festivals, carnivals, theatres, performance art centres and boasts one of the best local food shops in Wales, Feast of Food, in nearby Caersws. I was in the middle of the countryside but I was never exactly cut off from culture. Nowadays the Oriel Davies Gallery also serves some of the best coffee in Wales – and apart from books my other lifetime luxury item is good coffee. It's one of the three things in my view that you never compromise – the other two being butter and good loo roll!

I made plenty of lifelong friends in the town – Veronica and John Hollis and Christine Flemming, to name but three. In fact, my present-day life in mid-Wales would be totally impossible without Veronica. For over 25 years, she's been one of my best friends. She's a hugely talented (and busy!) person, who designs and builds houses and very kindly put all her work on hold to renovate mine.

Our time in Newtown was a whirl of picnics in our little white soft-top MG, windsurfing, long late dinner parties, fabulous conversations and a sense of extraordinary freedom. It was a blast of pure fresh air in every sense. Years later, when I returned to the area with Lembit, it was like coming home. I felt as if I fitted in from the start – I wish I could say the same about him.

Today I'm so glad I came back to mid-Wales even if it was with a man who would cause me so much grief! First time around I think I may have left the area too soon. It's funny how we all race from job to job when we're young. A year seems like a lifetime, staying in the same role for two years feels like stagnating…

Despite our blissful lives, Mark and I were soon on the move again. He was spending more and more time working in London and I was about to go on television.

'All you have to do is talk for a few minutes. How hard can that be?' It's difficult to be taken seriously as a continuity announcer on television. People think it's money for old rope but four minutes can be a very, very long time when you're on your own with just a cameraman in front of you and a stressed-out transmission controller shouting into your earpiece. Five minutes can feel like a lifetime.

I had come back to Cardiff to face just those challenges: on S4C, the Welsh-language version of Channel 4. I was one of four main presenters working alongside Siân Thomas, Nia Ceidiog and the evergreen Robin Jones. We worked out of the Sophia Close studios in the city centre, just off Cathedral Road, and I went onscreen within days of starting the job. Looking back, I know that going in front of the cameras for the first time should have been nerve-wracking and thrilling, but, naively perhaps, I never quite saw what all the fuss was about.

Having lived without a television throughout most of my childhood, I never quite got a sense of how important it was to the majority of other people. Sure, I was now working in the business but I still took it all with a huge pinch of salt. I didn't have that killer instinct, that over-arching desire to be famous. As usual, I was just coasting. People gave me opportunities because I didn't scare them with my ambition and because they knew I wouldn't make a fuss – I've always been a team player.

At first I did daytime continuity links, as well as the Children's Club programme in the afternoons but I was soon on the rota for some prime-time evening shifts as well. Unfortunately for my blood pressure, that was when you really earned your money as an announcer…

My first crisis came when I was leading in to Channel 4's 'In The Pink' season of gay films. I was only supposed to have 30 seconds to fill, but a computer fault at the network in Charlotte Street in London soon stretched this into three minutes. And, while that might not sound like much, every second crawls when you're fighting the clock. Try talking for three minutes about a single subject, especially without hesitation, deviation or repetition, and you'll see what I mean. It's like a high-pressure and very public game of *Just A Minute*.

Fortunately, I'd read the notes on the programmes carefully before going on air and just like in my exams I was able to picture the pages in my mind. I could remember enough facts to keep talking when the heat was on. The next time I was stretched was when I interviewed the channel's head of drama before a new show. In my radio days, I'd done plenty of recorded interviews but carrying out a high-profile interview live onscreen added another string to my bow. It could have been a bit of a bore but in fact it went brilliantly. I got some great answers from my guest and could probably have kept the interview going all night, if necessary. I loved it.

What I wasn't so sure about was being recognised in the street. By this time, I had bought my first house, a little place by the sea in Penarth, which cost me £25,000. I was always just 'Siân, from down the street' to my neighbours. I maintain you need to be on TV regularly for about three years before anyone notices you are there as a daily fixture and are going to stay. Ultimately, I lasted five years at S4C and by then I was already keen to move on again. This time I was heading back to London. My face was to get beamed around the world – and someone was going to offer me a job on the weather.

Chapter Six
Weather Girl

It all began at World Wide Television News (WWTN) in 1990. The TV news agency was based on Foley Street just north of Oxford Circus and very close to the BBC in Portland Place. ITN was just around the corner in Wells Street. It was yet another great place to put down foundations for the future. My department, Specials, produced strands and fillers for televisions stations around the world – I was being watched by millions of viewers in dozens of different countries, but no one in London knew who I was.

Part of my brief was to follow what happened in London and the UK and put it together for our global market. We had to look for big, iconic British stories that would play well overseas. One of my first stories came up when there were rumours that London Zoo was to be closed. I found some great library pictures, headed over there with a crew to film some more and presented a piece to camera on the story. Back at Foley Street, we edited it all together into a neat four-minute package. The finished product was hugely satisfying; I was in my element.

Next up came the mega-musical *Metropolis*. Millions of pounds had been spent on it, but it opened and closed in record time after some of the West End's most woeful reviews. I filmed a segment on all of that. I also covered fashion shows and sports events, and lots of light showbiz items.

We sold many of our strands to Brazilian and Japanese television stations. My dinners out with the Japanese executives were sometimes strange affairs but I got used to their very formal ways of mixing business with pleasure. A lot of my work also went out on Channel 9 in Australia. Dinners with the Aussies were a lot more relaxed.

The very big story I covered was the long-awaited release of the hostage John McCarthy on 8 August 1991. One of our staffers, he had been a captive in the Lebanon for more than five terrible years. As a constant reminder of his plight, we had a count of the number of days he had been in captivity in our reception. I headed over to RAF Lyneham to see him come out of the plane a free man. It was a huge, global story with the other crews from around the world jostling for position and trying to get the best angles. I thrived on it.

Back in Foley Street, I relished the time spent with some of my older colleagues. I loved hearing their tales of the glory days of broadcasting at ITN – even then there was a sense that these had long passed. Had it ever really been possible for newscasters in those not-so-long-ago times to get a taxi from the office on a Friday night and take it all the way to St Andrews for a weekend playing golf? Those were the kind of stories I lapped up in the office and wine bars after work. Even if the heyday of the industry had passed, it still felt like the coolest place to work. I got a buzz out of walking into our offices. My colleagues were intelligent, articulate and inspiring.

At this time, I was travelling from the West Country to London on a frequent basis, paying silly amounts for first-class tickets. Once I was doing the train journey during the period between Christmas and New Year and, as you'd expect, first class was virtually empty during that slow business period.

Standard, however, was very busy indeed, with people standing in the corridors. In Swindon, a little old lady was put on the train by her family. She was laden with Christmas gifts, so I helped her into the train and invited her to sit at my table. After all, there were no seats in standard class, and she had walking difficulties.

Along came the ticket inspector and promptly ordered her to go to standard class. I intervened, explaining she was disabled and had lots of parcels and anyway there was no room there. He barked at her to go there. I advised her to stay. She stayed; he lost his temper and threatened to call the police.

Lo and behold, as we drew into Reading Station, I saw a male and female police officer on the platform. They came on board to arrest me! Luckily for me, the male officer who was from Bridgend recognised me and laughed out loud, saying what a waste of police time the whole incident had been. He said he'd be filing a complaint about the inspector, wished the little old lady good luck and asked for my autograph!

Though I still had no long-term career plan, I loved being in a busy news environment where current affairs, campaigns and political issues were king. I thrived on controversial stories and breaking news. So how on earth did I end up on the weather?

In my capacity as specials producer for WWTN, I had been working with the Met Office. I'd especially enjoyed the company of John Charlesworth and Rex Roskilly. I'll happily admit I was dragged kicking and screaming by said gentlemen to my screen test at ITN. The weather seemed such a small sector. At that time, I thought it was just a peripheral issue. Surely the weather and the climate were never going to change? So why on earth would I want to limit myself to that?

I think I got the answer when I turned up at the ITN studios for my test. Like it or not, the weather suited me. Every bit of my experience to date – from school to work – had made me into the ideal candidate for the job. I offered three vital skills: I had an ability to take a brief quickly, I could make a good précis of vital information and I was able to carry on talking while all hell broke loose behind the scenes.

Dozens of people had a screen test. I think I was perhaps the only one who could keep talking sensibly for two minutes without drying up and remember all the key points and repeat them in a coherent manner. I had my presenting job at S4C to thank for that.

Of course, I did have a little bit of a head start. Way back on CBC in Cardiff I had already done weather reports as a rookie radio reporter. I covered storms and heat waves for

WWTN and even presented a five-minute-long farming forecast on S4C! On each occasion I was intrigued by the Met Office charts and tools – I liked the science behind the subject. Maybe it would be a good new challenge to really get to grips with it.

The more I thought about it, the more I realised the weather wasn't just an afterthought at the end of the news. It mattered to people – it still does and always will. Let's face it, the weather can be a matter of life and death. I remember at that time that I happened to be flicking through a book and found a fantastic quotation from Jerome K. Jerome claiming no one in Britain will ever be satisfied until they have their own personal weather forecaster. If so, I was never going to be out of work. The British were indeed obsessed with the weather!

In 1990, it was also clear that I could carve out my own niche if I did get the ITN job. Weather presenters were in a state of flux. Suzanne Charlton had just joined the BBC from the Met Office but it still retained plenty of grey-haired men and grandees. Meanwhile, channels like TV-am had its bright and bubbly new breed of viewer-friendly forecasters like Wincey Willis and new girl Ulrika Jonsson.

I was already 32 and in my case the whole glamour-girl thing didn't really interest me, but I was sure I could build a reputation between the two extremes. Having been so unwilling even to screen test for the ITN job, suddenly I became very keen to win it – and I did.

I resigned from WWTN and readied myself to enter a whole new world and as I did so I realised that once again I was living my life the wrong way round to almost everyone else. So many people in TV saw the weather as a stepping stone to more mainstream television. For them it was a foot in the door, not a destination in its own right. But after my time in Foley Street I felt I had done plenty of mainstream, general-interest TV already and I was happy to specialise. Being a jack-of-all-trades is fun but I was ready to become master of just one.

In my early days on the weather, most of my broadcasts were live but then everything about the job was a baptism of fire. At the start of each shift, I sat down with our regular forecasters and meteorologists. We pored over the charts and faxes from the Met Office, which contained information such as wind speeds, temperatures and levels of rainfall, to draw up some rough charts for our teams of graphic artists. Mid-afternoon every day was sacrosanct. It was time for the day's national conference calls held by the Met Office. These were like being on a giant party line and anyone on it, from Lands End to John O'Groats, could speak out and give details or ask questions about their particular area. The experts at the other end were based at Met Office HQ, then in Bracknell and now in Exeter. I lapped it all up.

In weather forecasting, as in so many other aspects of modern life, it's the advance in computing power that has been responsible for the most dramatic changes over the last 15 years. Satellites are now far more sophisticated and can give us a much more detailed picture of what the weather is doing right now. That information is fed into computer models that are now so detailed that a forecast for three days ahead is as accurate as a 24-hour forecast was 15 years ago.

Within a matter of months of starting on the weather, I

discovered something else about myself: I found the whole subject endlessly and genuinely interesting. The technology and the mathematics and the computing that turn the Met Office's observations into forecasts were fascinating. And so my long-dormant puritanical streak reared its head again.

I started to feel conscious of how arts and language based my education and qualifications were. Science was a huge gap in my knowledge base and it had to be filled. What I also wanted was credibility with viewers, but more importantly with the Met Office staff I dealt with every day.

The British Met Office is the world's best – it's as simple as that. Its staff, its systems, its accuracy couldn't be more impressive. And I respect people at the top of their fields. I was surrounded by professionals daily and I wanted to prove I had a right to work alongside them, so I decided to get qualified.

I spoke to my boss, the ever-inspirational John Charlesworth, and he persuaded the Met Office to set up a course for presenters who had a journalistic background. I would be the guinea pig to test it out. I did day-release learning, with lectures at the old Met Office College in Shinfield, near Bracknell. There I learned how to read the charts properly, do the calculations and appreciate the physics and chemical side to forecasting. John Charlesworth played a pivotal role. He was the one who originally persuaded me to screen test for the job and he tailor-made my meteorological course. Afterwards, he often joked that they made the course a lot easier after my day!

With Mark by my side at home, I had another scientist

to hand if I struggled with anything, though I remember he wasn't always as sympathetic as I would have liked him to be.

'What do you mean, you don't understand what "mass" means?' he asked me, exasperated, one evening.

'I'm a Classicist! The idea of "mass" didn't exactly arise,' I replied, whacking him with my textbook.

But the gear change was well worth it and Mark's guidance certainly helped. I passed my exams first time and got my qualification. Following this, I felt I could look everyone in the eye at work. I'm probably prouder of that qualification than any other.

Of course, being able to pull a forecast together is only one part of the presenter's job. The other challenge is to get it across to viewers. The weather is one of the few parts of the television industry that doesn't use autocues; we have to remember everything and make sure we time our words right down to the very last second. The Production Assistants (PAs) are counting us into the broadcast, and down to the end through our earpieces. Apart from that, we are pretty much on our own.

And, of course, we really can't see the map we are pointing to. The screen behind me at ITN used to be blue, now it's green. Cameras project the map on to it through what's known as a Colour Separation Overlay (CSO) system, but I can't see it. It means that when I turn to look at the map during a broadcast all I see is the green felt wall. The only time I can see the map is when I'm not looking at it: when I look ahead at the camera or the monitor to the side. Everything is topsy-turvy and the wrong way round, which may be another reason why doing the weather suits my life. It's a bit like patting your head and rubbing your stomach at the same time. I often think that if a Martian looked down on me in the studio he wouldn't have a clue what was going on. He would see a lone woman, talking into space and pointing at something that isn't there. I'm well aware I've got one of the strangest jobs around.

Life in front of the weather chart plays havoc with certain hairstyles. CSO can cause a seriously bad hair day if you're not careful; any stray bits of hair open a gateway to the weather chart seeping through. As I'm presenting the weather in front of a chart with a green light, having a halo or green flecks in your hair is definitely not a flattering look! Flicks and curls that look good in everyday life are just disastrous onscreen. And, believe me, viewers are quick to complain about what they think is a messy hairstyle, when in reality it is the weather chart that is distorting the image.

Over time, all weather presenters learn plenty of tricks to make our trade easier. People often comment on the way I use my hands and fingers when I point to the maps. The *Guardian* even published an article about it, likening my hands to an Indian dancer! But, when you can't see anything other than a blue or green felt wall, you can't afford to be too specific. If you point at a single, static spot you have to be absolutely clear that the weather you are talking about will hit right there. And on a national broadcast of less than two minutes you need to talk in broader brushstrokes. A big sweep of the hand covers a multitude of meteorological sins.

The clothes we wear are just as important. There has

always been a vague ITN look, as elegantly personified by Mary Nightingale nowadays and Selina Scott in the old days, and I guess I'm more or less in line with them. The practical rules are that you can't wear checks or patterns because they will shimmer and shake onscreen. You couldn't wear blue in my early days and I can't wear green now because, if I did, the map would show up on my body through the CSO system! We have never been given a clothes allowance at ITN but over the years I managed to build up some classics. I keep some nice Paul Smith and Armani and Jill Sander jackets at the office. But the old Chelsea Girl and Biba-lover in me always tries to wake things up with something a little more funky like a bold piece of jewellery.

Looking good on TV is a must for any female presenter. Luckily, I have always paid attention to personal grooming and am a firm believer that looking good makes you feel good. I also like to take care of my health and have the energy to live life to the full.

I'm often asked if there is added pressure on me to stay in shape because of my career on TV. The reality for any female on TV is that you *are* judged by your appearance and your age. The lovely Moira Stewart left the BBC amid claims of ageism, despite a campaign by Jeremy Paxman, David Frost and Terry Wogan. Female presenters, however professional and good they are at their job, are scrutinised in a way that their male counterparts are not. Of course, this type of sexism is unfair, but it can be found in numerous professions. Sadly it's often women who call to complain if they don't like what you're wearing, don't like your hairstyle or think you're overweight.

Juggling a busy schedule means time is very much at a

premium. Over the years, I've fine-tuned my health and beauty regime to fit in with my lifestyle. I simply don't have the time or the inclination to spend hours in a beauty salon being pampered. Other than my nails, which really do benefit from a professional manicure, I like treatments that are fast, effective and don't require me to spend hours in the bathroom or demand a whole suitcase of products.

I spend a lot of time travelling and I've become a dab hand at packing and unpacking. I select a capsule wardrobe and only take the essential personal-care products with me to any location. At home, my bathroom cabinet is surprisingly sparse and friends are often surprised that it's not overflowing with lotions and potions. Equally, I don't have a drawer full of unused make-up and impulse buys. This is largely down to the fact that over the years I have picked up lots of tricks of the trade and am lucky enough to be able to call on the experts to select the best products and treatments for me.

Sometimes I can be in the strangest of places, anywhere from a city-centre boutique to a Scottish charity shop, when suddenly I see a jacket that I know will be perfect for television. Either way, I'll rush to buy it. One of my favourite jackets from the early days came from a tiny shop in Inverness. Others originate from trips to Sydney, which I visited to write a travel piece for the *Mail on Sunday*, or to Paris when I visit Ceri. If I see something that will work, I have to have it.

So, as the 1990s got under way I couldn't have been happier. My love life with Mark was still good, my career fulfilling, I was very relaxed... Which led to my first big onscreen disaster.

A FUNNY KIND OF LOVE

It happened on the lunchtime news. I was working in ITN's old Wells Street studio and the whole set-up and structure of the show was very different from how it is today. My role as weather presenter was to say a few words alongside the main news anchor at the start of the show. Then I left the news desk and just stood by until I gave my full report at the end of the programme. I think John Suchet was on with me on this particular day and everything seemed to be proceeding as normal. Normal, that is, until all of his live links started to break down.

The producers had me standing by to go on early if they couldn't raise a tape for John's third story but they stood me down when the replacement story started to play. Then it happened again. A video couldn't be played so we were about to move to the weather – then we weren't. I was up and down, up and down, for what felt like the full half-hour.

Just before going on camera I would always chew some gum and have a quick drink of water. It's just a habit I've got into. The peppermint burst from the gum always makes me feel more awake and ready for action, and the water makes sure my mouth isn't too dry. On this particular day, the producers told me I had 30 seconds to go, so I chewed and drank as usual. Then it was a panic. Something else had gone wrong and Alastair was handing over to me then and there. I went live to the nation chewing a piece of gum and holding a glass of water in my left hand: the hand I needed to point to the map.

'Good afternoon,' I said, with my biggest smile and the gum under my tongue. *Please* don't let it slip out of the side of my mouth! I knew there was nothing I could do about the glass. I couldn't lean down to put it on the floor and there was no one to hand it to. But I could do something about the gum... I turned to the map – the blank green screen behind me. In a split second, hoping my face was obscured from the camera, I spit out the gum. It wasn't exactly ladylike. My mother, let alone dear Mrs O.G. from chapel and Mrs Powell from school, would have been horrified. But for a split second I thought I'd got away with it. I smiled again, faced the camera and clicked on to the next screen to start my review.

When I looked ahead towards the camera, I could see the map and it looked fine. But, when I turned to point at it, I noticed there was a problem: I spat my gum a little too hard. It had attached itself to the felt wall and was sticking out just where I would imagine Cornwall to be. When I faced forward again and looked at the monitor, I couldn't tell if the blip was visible – it was too small a screen and it was too far away, but I had a horrible feeling eagle-eyed viewers would have noticed it. I always smile a lot during my broadcasts and I always try to sign off with a positive 'Good Afternoon' or 'Good Night'. This time it couldn't have been more heartfelt. The moment I was counted out by the PA, I nearly fell over laughing.

Fortunately, the whole production team were in stitches as well and I had my first bit of media interest. I was asked to go on *Tomorrow's World* to help film a feature about the tastes of different types of chewing gum. And then I was even approached to do a chewing-gum ad but in those days we were not allowed to. Clearly I had arrived!

Warm smiles, broad hand gestures and chewing gum apart, I remained deadly serious about my job. I've always believed it has to be grounded in the science. I see it as information, not entertainment, and you need to get across as much as your tiny time slot allows. I would be driven mad if I was watching the weather and the presenter waffled rather than told me what I needed to know, so I try to get as many facts into my forecasts as possible.

It's also worth noting how important the weather is to us all. It's not just about clothes and our social lives, and whether or not we should carry an umbrella, important as those things are. Supermarkets need to know what the weekends are going to be like so they can decide what kind of food to stock, whether they should bring in extra burger buns and steaks for barbecues on hot summer weekends or if they will need extra soup and anti-freeze for cold snaps. Councils want to know when to commit themselves to the expensive business of sending out road-gritters. The weather matters to us in Britain: as an island, we're buffeted from all sides. And, let's face it, where would our conversations be if we didn't have the weather to talk about? It's at the heart of our national life. That's why I've never fallen out of love with it.

After nearly three years in the job, I felt at home. Based on my career moves to date this should have been the time when I moved on to pastures new. But this time I didn't want to. A bit of real recognition also kept me in the job. In 1993, I was flown over to Paris to collect the Presenter's Award at the International Weather Forecasters' Festival. It was an incredible accolade especially since I was chosen by all the other weather presenters from around the world and I was thrilled to have been voted for it. Life couldn't be better, could it?

When I first started out on the weather, I moved into the best house-share in London. I lived on Elgin Crescent in Holland Park, West London, with two wonderful Welsh friends. They were friends who would ensure our house was the best connected and the most energising in town.

Karl Francis and I had met years earlier at the BBC in Wales. My twin claim to fame was first that my mum and I had come up with the name for one of his controversial films and that I had won a bit part in another of them. He had been telling me all about the as-yet untitled production and later that day I was chatting about it with my mum. Suddenly, we hit upon the phrase 'Boy Soldier' as the perfect title. Karl agreed. It was a translation of the title of a popular Welsh hymn, *Milwr Bychan*, and I was proud of my mum for coming up with it.

My second claim to fame – I used to joke that it was my big Hollywood break – was that I played a newsreader in his film about the miners' strike. If you watch *Ms Rhymney Valley* and don't cough at the vital moment, you will hear me on a television screen in the background. I acted my heart out. But the Best Supporting Actress award at the Oscars went elsewhere that year. Good job I never wrote a speech!

Kim Howells was the third member of our West London household. After moving on from journalism and the media in Wales, he had become Labour MP for Pontypridd in 1989. All told, the three of us covered a lot of bases, from politics through filmmaking to television. It meant our home turned into some kind of modern-day salon, with a guest book to match.

I could leave my tiny little box-room one morning to

find the American producer of the Cohen brothers' films asleep on the sofa of our living room. The next morning a politician or union friend of Kim's might be staying with us. Then someone from ITN or one of our regional offices would need a sofa for the night. It was eclectic, exciting and invigorating. I felt as if I was at the heart of so many important events. We truly were in the fifth estate and I thrived on getting to know all these different sorts of people. It didn't matter if they were from politics, the film world or television: they were an extraordinary array of characters, many of international standing with the horizons to match. I thought I was grown up already but I grew up so much more in my Holland Park years. I'm not dazzled by showbiz, but I am by the most impressive people and their minds.

In our Holland Park house Karl, Kim and I proved something else that has always been important to me, something I could never quite get across to Lembit when our relationship got under way. It was that you don't need booze to have a good time. Karl doesn't drink, so most of the time Kim and I didn't either. Neither of us missed it. Elgin Crescent was still a great place to be. Our fun was generated by strong personalities and opinions and not alcohol. Karl, in fact, made what I regard as the definitive film on alcoholism, *The Happy Alcoholic*, starring Dafydd Hywel.

On the political front, I loved hearing Kim's amazing stories from the House of Commons. Often Karl and I would stay up to wait for him to come home after an important vote. We were keen to know who had said what in the chamber and in the corridors; we wanted the inside track and the gossip, and it was incredible to have a window on this world. John Major had taken over as Prime Minister and was about to fight his first election. Politics was exciting and raw back then. We couldn't have had a better housemate than Kim.

Best of all, Mark was just as comfortable in my metropolitan new world, though based in Wiltshire for work purposes. For a long time our relationship motored on as relaxed and happy as ever. Our long-distance living arrangements didn't bother either of us for years; we never quite lived and worked in the same place at the same time for very long but we were always ready to travel to make sure we didn't become strangers. Sometimes it felt as if we had three homes between the two of us: our old house in Penarth, my flat-share in London and The Old Malthouse down in Wiltshire. Bouncing between them all was part of the fun. I enjoyed feeling like a slightly different person in each location.

Recently someone asked me why in all that time Mark and I never got married. I can say quite truthfully that the subject never really mattered to us. We were in that peer group for whom marriage wasn't the be-all and end-all of life; we were never in a phase where we spent every weekend at friends' weddings and were pushed into considering our own. There's that classic line in the film *Four Weddings and a Funeral* where Simon Callow's character says that many couples decide to get married when they run out of things to say to each other. Mark and I never stopped talking; we always had things to say. Our relationship worked, we were happy and the topic never really cropped up.

In a funny kind of way, I think I can also blame my job

for my disinterest in marriage. Back in the early days of ITN, we had hair and make-up staff to fuss over us before every broadcast (costcutting means we're now on our own). Coupled with guest appearances on shows like *Cluedo*, *Richard and Judy*, *Go Getters*, *The Clothes Show* and the like, I'd already enjoyed lots of Big Days! I didn't need a wedding to make me feel the centre of attention.

The other subject that never arose between Mark and me was trust. We continued to be absolutely secure in each other's fidelity. So right through the first half of the 1990s, we couldn't have been luckier. Perhaps that luck couldn't last forever. Maybe long-distance relationships always cool faster than the average. Whatever the reason, as the years passed I think Mark and I did start to edge off in slightly different directions. Everyone changes subtly over the years and by 1995 I think Mark and I both knew our love affair was over.

I was in the process of moving out of the Holland Park house into my own flat in Marylebone when we parted. It felt like the right time to make the break. There was no drama and no betrayals, just as there hadn't been when I had split with Siôn before university. To be honest, Mark and I hardly needed to talk about what was happening. It felt organic and easy, and it played out very comfortably over several months. Best of all, while our love affair died, our friendship lives on. Today Mark and I speak on the phone all the time. We go on treks together, see each other at frequent house parties and share the best of memories.

Of course, there's always a sadness when something comes to an end, but, when that something has already dropped a gear to friendship over a period of time, then there's no horrible hurt as such. I spent a long time with Mark and was very happy. In a way, I grew up with him and part of what I am today is hugely influenced by him. I will always be grateful for his honesty, politeness, responsibility, willingness to share and openness.

Interestingly enough, my next long-term relationship would also end in a mature adult fashion. I met Greg Tosh through friends in the mid-1990s. He was a cameraman and one of the nicest, most reliable and kindest men I have met. My friends adored him. In many ways, I saw him as the Scottish version of Mark. No wonder we were drawn to each other. He will always be one of my best friends in the whole world.

Greg was always so welcoming and so interested in what everyone was doing. His great gift to me was the love of hill-walking and trekking. He was young and passionate about the outdoors and when we went on our first big hikes I could see why. I was leading a metropolitan life but I have always craved contrasts. Hill-walking provided them. I'm not a spiritual person but those first long treks I did with Greg took me into a calmer, freer place. Tough walks do the same for me today. When I hike, it's the closest I come to communing with anything. And, hey, treks also gave me a great bum and legs! I didn't get named Rear of the Year in 2007 – at 49 – because of hours spent on some treadmill in a gym. It was all down to being out in the open air and pounding the trails.

Hiking with Greg taught me to value peace and space. I realised in London I was always surrounded by people and noise. The solitude we found in the mountains was invigorating; it balanced me. As a proud Scot, Greg also taught me how to ski. He had the patience of Job! I hit my first slopes amid the icy gales of Glenshee – and I maintain today that, if you can ski there, you can ski anywhere. We often stayed with his wonderful parents on the outskirts of Dundee. They welcomed me into their family with such warmth and enthusiasm. They are typical Scottish salt-of-the-earth folk and Greg inherited their sweetness and generosity.

For my birthday one year, he booked the spectacular Altnaharrie Inn, which is situated on an isolated peninsula up towards the north-west of Scotland. A water taxi took us to this stunning, peaceful place, where I had one of the best meals of my life. Breakfast the next morning was magnificent. This is an example of the kind and thoughtful man Greg is. Another time we took the sleeper train from Euston to Inverness on the night of my birthday. As a surprise, he put together a wonderful hamper, stuffed with champagne, walnut bread, cold meats and cheeses, pickles and chutneys, chocolate and raspberry tart, and petits fours. I was in heaven!

Greg's job meant he was away a huge amount of the time – if he wasn't setting up a satellite transmission system in Africa, he might be filming in a battle zone in the Gulf. It was literally a case of Kazakhstan one week, the Philippines the next. He was a brilliant cameraman and organiser. He sometimes found himself in tricky situations, once with the Georgian mafia, another time with a knife-wielding thief in Johannesburg. His cool, calm and collected presence meant he always pulled through. He won an award for bravery when filming in the Gulf during the first war.

Greg would move heaven and earth to keep in touch, using a satellite phone from the middle of the Russian plains or a remote island in the Pacific. When he was in London, he lived in Primrose Hill, while I was still in my flat over in Marylebone. We never lived together because we never felt the need. Neither of us was insecure. When our relationship ended after some six comfortable years, it followed the same pattern as before. There was a natural drawing to a close of things and we became more like brother and sister. I remember my times with him and the rest of the Scottish gang with huge fondness and no regret at all. It was a brilliant, active, life-enhancing period and I'm lucky to have been so closely involved with such a lovely man. We both agreed that we were heading in slightly different directions and we shared a simple acceptance about what had to be done. When you don't have children to worry about, and you have plenty of joint friends to offer you support, I think you can move on amicably and as adults.

Being single has never bothered me, not least because I work so hard to keep my friendships alive. Today I am close to people I grew up with and worked with back in Wales, like Novello Noades, Veronica Hollis and Stifyn Parri. But I also love the fact that you can make wonderful new friends in the most unlikely of settings. I think I can tell almost straight away when I meet someone with whom I'm going to connect.

For instance, I met my good friend Astrid Kearny at the Clarin's beauty counter in Fenwick's on Bond Street. Within a few weeks, she was working with us on the weather and is now one of the most sought-after make-up artists and stylists in the country. How lucky we are!

In my early weather years, I went up to Hampstead to the salon of a beauty therapist called Eileen Mulligan. We got talking, instantly connected and I thought she was the kind of person who could be a friend for life. I was right. Over the years, we have both been through a lot but we have always been the best of friends and can always rely on each other.

Back in the 1990s, I wanted to look as good as possible because I was starting to gain a much higher profile. It could have been my chewing-gum moment, perhaps it was the awards I was winning or it might just have been that I was riding the weather-girl wave. Whatever the reason I started to be invited to appear on lots of other television shows. I still didn't watch a lot of TV so I frequently didn't know what I had let myself in for, but if it sounded fun then I would give it a go. That's my philosophy on life, after all.

Most of those early, one-off appearances are totally forgettable today. But many of the people I met have stuck in my mind. Two key examples are Jerry Hall and Joanna Lumley, both of whom I encountered on an episode of a game show called *Cluedo*. It was one of my first ventures beyond the comfort zone of my weather studio and in small, but different ways both my co-stars taught me lessons about good behaviour. Jerry was friendly to everyone. I remember this extraordinarily tall, angular figure rushing towards me in the Green Room. 'Hi Siân, I'm Jerry,' she said, stretching out a perfectly manicured hand. And despite her Texan accent she pronounced my name just right – which a lot of other people still struggle to do.

Joanna was even more relaxed and gracious. I think she has had such a long and successful career because she has never got stressed or paranoid about it or wanted it too much. She seemed to enjoy every moment of her time on set, but I got the impression she would have been just as happy walking down a country lane. She was grounded and had a life beyond the cameras.

Over the years, I have worked with many other people who pay cuttings agencies so they can see every word that is ever written about them. I've never really got this. All I have is a Selfridges' bag in a cupboard stuffed with a few old magazines and torn newspaper articles. Most of those are things my friends have posted to me or a journo in ITN may have spotted in one of the papers. The truth is, I've never taken any of these things too seriously. In the great scheme of things, it means nothing.

It's the same with my telly work. I never sat flicking through the television channels or going through the weekly listings saying, 'Whey didn't I get that gig?' or 'Why is she on that when they could have had me?' In recent years, one of the few programmes I would have relished was *Britain's Favourite View* – I would have killed to put a case for the view of Cader Idris! And I guess the only presenters I really envy are Griff Rhys Jones and Michael Palin – give me their jobs any day!

Other than that, I think I do what Joanna does: I turn up, do the most professional job I can, enjoy it and I never know what might come up tomorrow. When you live like this, tomorrow tends to look after itself.

I proved this by winning the role of co-presenter on the children's television programme *How2* in 1997 when Carol Vorderman left the show. We recorded it up in Glasgow for STV and had a lot of laughs with the wonderful Fred Dinenage and his co-presenter Gareth Jones (Gaz Top). My scientific background appealed to the producer, and I loved working in such a demanding role – there was no autocue and reams of complicated information to remember. Once again, my memory held me in good stead.

I also followed Carol on to a few special editions of *Countdown* and had a real laugh with Paul O'Grady's Lily Savage on *Blankety Blank*. I went on almost anything Noel Edmonds was presenting; back then his dominance of the Saturday-night light-entertainment market was complete. Some of the programmes are more stressful but, since I've been lucky enough never to have had nerves, you're basically earning good money for a lot of fun. And the reason I never really got nervous was that I never take things too seriously, so I've been very lucky through the years. I've appeared on most of the big shows from *This Morning* to *Ant and Dec*, *Breakfast with Frost* to *Dimbleby* and *This Week*.

It was lunchtime and I was sitting at my desk at work having a sandwich when he came over.

'Siân?' he said.

'Yes?'

I looked up, smiling. But I stopped when he said his name. This man had been writing to me for weeks. He had been penning increasingly bad, angry letters. And now he had somehow got through security and made it right up to my desk.

I looked around our huge open-plan office in North London's Camden Lock but there was no one in sight. It was the day the whole lunchtime team seemed to have gone shopping or to the canteen at the same time. Everything went very slowly.

'Can I help you?' I asked. Maybe I had misheard his name; perhaps this wasn't him. He might just be a contractor sent over to fix the computers.

'Did you get my letters? I sent you letters.'

So it *was* him; I was unnaturally calm. This was long before Jill Dando's death, but some other high-profile cases of stalkers had shaken up the whole of the broadcasting industry. Everyone felt vulnerable, especially the women. How could this man have got through security?

'I'm not sure if I got your letters. What's your name again?' I was stalling for time and desperately hoping I could keep him sweet until someone else came into the room. He repeated his name and mentioned a meeting place he said I should have gone to. And he was at the edge of my desk, far too close. He could reach out and touch me.

I was trying to work out if I could stand up or if this would trigger a bad reaction. In many ways, he was an indeterminate man. I couldn't quite place his age, his accent, anything about him. If you passed him in the street, you would barely notice him. Perhaps that's what had made him so angry. But why had he put the focus of that anger on me?

Our faltering conversation went on. I was desperately wishing we had some sort of panic alarms on our desks, the kind they have in banks. But why would we? Why would you ever be in danger in your place of work?

It was then that our big burly director Simon Morris arrived back in the office. My visitor clearly stood out as a stranger; my body language must have shown he was unwelcome. I flashed a glance across the room and Simon moved forward. He too was well aware of all the recent stories about stalkers and he wasn't going to take any chances.

Everything suddenly sped up as Simon manhandled the stranger away from me. Finally, our security staff arrived to help and a rush of other colleagues appeared from nowhere to check I was OK. Then it was over.

I tried to blot out the follow-up, not wanting to know what the police might or might not be doing to stop this happening again. I assumed if they had any worries they would tell me. Instead, I relied on my gut feeling that told me the man had been angry, not violent. He had built me up as a fantasy figure. Now he had met me, up close and personal, he *must* know the game was over. I would never meet him in any of his prearranged locations. In my soul, I believed he would move on.

And anyway, it wasn't as if this was the first time I'd had problems. I had long since learned that bad letters to people in the public eye tend to follow a pattern. First, they ask to meet you at a certain place and time. Then they want to know why you weren't there. They suggest an alternative; they're very specific. Then they say you can have one more chance. Then they get very angry. At this point a tiny number become frighteningly sexual, listing exactly what they want to do. Others disturb in other ways. They say, 'I love you, I love you, I love you,' on every line of every page – and they run to more than a dozen pages.

Other people say they hear voices that tell them to write in and that we need to meet. Sometimes I get their wedding or holiday photos – with their wives' heads cut out and replaced by mine. Sometimes, of course, I receive other pictures, pictures that certainly weren't taken in any church.

Another man once delivered a frightening letter to my old home in Cardiff. That shook me up just as much as the visit to our newsroom. And I had a phone stalker in the early days at S4C as well. It was someone who rang me at 4am to talk dirty – *very* dirty. It took me a while to work out how anyone could have my number. Then I suddenly guessed he might have been one of the builders who had been working on my house. 'I'll tell your boss what you are doing,' I said, on one early-morning call. It was the weakest of threats, but it did the trick because he never called again.

It's the price we pay for being in the public eye. My friend Lucy Owen, who now hosts *Wales Today* in Cardiff, was in a similar situation, and then of course there was Billie Piper, among others like Madonna and Princess Diana. After my office experience, I did a special on stalkers for *Tonight with Trevor McDonald*. It's not something anyone can ever trivialise but you can't let it rule your life. And on those rare occasions when I do get hassle, I think of all the good letters that outnumber the bad a thousand times over.

People write to ask where I get my lip-gloss or who does my hair. They want to know where I bought my jacket. Lovely, lonely older ladies tell me all about their days. Kids want to know how the screens work, media students ask for work experience and tips on finding their first jobs. Dads write in saying their daughters are getting married in eight months' time and do I think the weather will behave if they book a marquee for the reception.

Years ago, most television studios had staff who helped answer all our post. Those days are now long gone and like most presenters I struggle to see everything that comes in. It's the same being approached in the street. Often I don't get recognised because the glossy me onscreen can be very different from the sleepy one in my combats and baseball cap, who buys the morning papers and a pint of milk! Nor, sadly, am I overwhelmed with gifts from designers: evening clothes are always a problem as I do so much work attending charity functions, so it's a good job I like hitting the shops. I've always quite enjoyed chatting to people when I'm out and about – I regard it as part and parcel of my job.

From the late-1990s onwards the fun was about to move up a gear. On the steps of BBC Television Centre in West London, I was about to meet a man who had recently swapped a role in *Brookside* as Christopher Duncan for the part of Marius in the West End production of *Les Miserables*. Soon my new best friend Stifyn Parri and I were laughing so much I had to start buying waterproof mascara. Good times were about to roll.

Chapter Seven
Happy Days

I call Stifyn my scriptwriter. Many's the time I remember one of his most brilliant lines or anecdotes and claim it as my own. And I'm not the only one. I was taking part in a big primetime network BBC1 show a few years ago when I heard Michael Ball tell a hilarious story that sounded very familiar. Back in the mid-eighties Michael was Stifyn's flat-mate in Aberystwyth. It seemed as if he knew a good line when he heard one as well.

Fooling around for the BBC's *Comic Relief* brought us together. Food kept us close, too. We are both inveterate foodies. Often he might be driving from Cardiff to London as I'm driving the other way. The entire way we can be on our mobiles discussing the meals we have just eaten.

'So were there pine nuts on it?'

'Yes, and they had toasted the...'

'And was it...'

And so it goes on – for the entire duration of the M4.

We both speak Welsh and have the same take on life, sharing the same sense of humour. Both of us are fiercely proud of our country. But we always thought the Welsh were marginalised; it seemed wrong that the Irish and the Scots should always get so much attention. Didn't everyone know how sexy we are in Wales?!

'Maybe the world doesn't know,' I said once.

'Well, let's tell them.'

So Stifyn decided to set up a club for Welsh ex-pats and friends: Social Welsh Sexy or *Sws* ('kiss' in Welsh). And the main part of the logo that's on our website and all our promotional material comes from a very famous kiss. The lipstick and the lips belong to Catherine Zeta Jones, one of our highest-profile supporters. She kissed a white handkerchief for us and Stifyn had it immortalised. Other big names were just as happy to join our new gang.

I was named after the Welsh actress Siân Phillips – she had been my mother's roommate at university and I've always admired her. She hosted the opening party at the Groucho Club in London on 26 November 1995. Exactly 40 people had been invited and exactly 40 of us turned up. And what a party it was!

I think that until SWS came along most Londoners' idea of a Welsh evening would probably have involved a cake contest and a clog dance. We knocked all that on the head fast. The Irish could carry on having a wild *craic*; we would show that it was just as good when the Welsh had a *hwyl*.

Colin Jackson, Ioan Gruffudd, Bonnie Tyler and Bryn Terfel are just some of our well-known members, but we have very many more from all walks of life – you don't even need to be Welsh to take part. You just have to share our spirit and sense of adventure.

Today SWS has members and local groups around the world – we've even got a group in Moscow. On St David's Day in 1999, we had 500 people at our New York opening, with what felt like a similar number of paparazzi outside hoping to get a shot of the soon-to-be-married Catherine Zeta Jones.

From New York, I flew over to LA for yet another incredible opportunity. As a member of the Wales Tourist Board, I was helping to promote our country as an ideal place for film locations. I hosted some glitzy receptions in Hollywood and had Catherine's brothers David and Lyndon as my off-duty tour guides to LA. It was heady stuff.

Back in London, Stifyn and I would sometimes go out three or four nights a week. Today all I remember of those times is laughing and laughing, event after event, party after party. At a big formal bash for the French Ambassador, I ended up sitting next to Lord Puttnam. Cinema is one of my passions, so I couldn't have been happier. And, with so many high-profile politicians, opinion-formers and arts bosses around, the conversation was quite extraordinary.

We had temporarily moved on from the future of independent film, third-world-debt relief and all our other detailed discussions.

'Yes, I like to make my own muesli,' I announced to Lord Puttnam, just as silence descended on the table. It was one of those moments when everyone fell silent all at once. To this day, I have never been able to forget it.

'You were surrounded by world leaders and arts

impresarios, and you're telling David Puttnam that you chop your own almonds every morning and then throw in a handful of raisins,' Stifyn jokes. 'I don't think if any of them knew what hit them, though I must say, they seemed more interested in your special muesli recipe than anything else being discussed!'

Another surreal incident came about at Buckingham Palace. I was helping at a reception and presentation for the Duke of Edinburgh Awards scheme. In a break after my part of the ceremony was over, I went for a short walk in the gardens. The palace lawns are pristine – or at least they were until I strolled across them in spiked three-inch high heels! Looking back, I probably didn't do the carpets and the parquet flooring any favours either. I don't think the Queen is a great high-heel wearer. Not my finest hour, but then I always was a faint-hearted monarchist.

Friends and family certainly approved of the Siân and Stifyn show. After a broadcast, I would get calls. 'You're wearing your hair up and dangly earrings – you two must be going out for a big party tonight,' I'd be told. More often than not they were right. They were such enjoyable times, the only times when I operated on the fringes of the whole showbiz thing. Stifyn and I would hang out with everyone from rock stars to the cast of *EastEnders*. Week after week we had our photographs in the *Western Mail* – readers probably thought we were living the ultimate sex, drugs and rock'n'roll lifestyle. In truth, it was none of the above. I'm still the queen of making one glass of champagne last all night – Lembit used to hate that about me. But less is more in my book.

I'm always too excited about what might be happening

tomorrow to waste a second of time on a hangover. Drugs are something I have always hated. In fact, I have an abhorrence of them. I don't want to be in another place – my life is fun enough, after all. Thankfully, I've never gone through the dreadful experience of knowing a drug addict, or someone whose life was destroyed by drugs. But I do remember that, when I was about nine, my auntie Carol came to visit and my mother took a cigarette from her. She never smoked and I guess this was a one-off. I was so terribly upset that I ran upstairs to her bedroom and wrote CANCER in pink lipstick across the dressing-table mirror!

In those merry years I think my next best moment came the night Stifyn and I snubbed Elton John. We were in the South of France. Stifyn was producing a huge party at the Cannes Film Festival and we were staying with friends, Hilary and Roy King (aka the Bear), who run a theatre company in Antibes. We were in their incredible house on the Cap, with its lavish gardens, pool and exquisite furnishings. There, we spent lazy days lounging around the pool with Hilary and the Bear, chilling and laughing, and eating exquisite food, generally having a ball.

Then Stifyn got the call: Elton was holding a housewarming party up in the hills. The guest list was stellar, just as you might expect. It would be the biggest party of the year.

'But we can't go. We can't let Hilary down,' I said.

'Is the meal tonight?' Stifyn asked.

It was. Hilary's adorable Vietnamese cook was preparing a Welsh feast in our honour. For weeks she had been researching it and preparing for days. That had to come first and we never made it to Elton's, though we did hear on the grapevine that everyone was given the most incredible goodie bags when they left.

Back in London we weren't exactly out of circulation. And we got to see parts of the stars that others don't get to see. We went to lots of the *An Audience With* recordings at the old LWT Tower on London's South Bank. A double high came on Shirley Bassey's sixtieth birthday show. The main thing I remember of that night is that Stifyn, shame on him, stole one of the candles from Dame Shirley's birthday cake. The only mitigating circumstance is that he lifted it after the lady had blown them all out and swept on out of the room.

Next thing I remember was Stifyn's face as he rushed back from the gents just before we were ushered over to our seats.

'What are you so excited about?'

'Siân, you will never guess.'

'What is it?'

'Guess who I stood next to having a pee.'

I had absolutely no idea. But Stifyn answered anyway.

'Tom Jones! *Only* Tom *bloody* Jones! So of course I had to look.'

And I *had* to know.

'It's huge. Like a fallen tree, like Blackpool log flume!'

Needless to say, the pair of us giggled and gossiped our way through most of the remaining evening. But the fun wasn't over.

Dame Shirley did an extraordinary set – all sung live, no lip-syncing. At the end of the show, she gave us a real showstopper of a final number. And in the last moments she gave the biggest – and most extended – high kick I had ever seen. Stifyn and I were at the closest table to the stage, with a direct view of everything. And it turned out that Shirley wasn't wearing any knickers. So, when I say everything, I mean *everything*.

On the way out of the studio, Stifyn rang his mother: 'Mam, tonight I've seen Tom Jones's *bleep* and Shirley Bassey's *bleep*!'

'Oh, you *are* having a good night!' she responded.

We left the building, the pair of us weak with laughter.

One more story of all those frothy times and it's an important one because it introduced me to the world of charity treks. I do a lot of work for NCH, the old National Children's Homes charity, which now does so much more than simply offering refuge to at-risk youngsters. I'm now a vice president. Over the years, my other main charities have included Mencap, Scope, Breakthrough Breast Cancer, Marie Curie and the Hospice movement. Breakthrough asked me, together with a selection of other supporters, to attend the opening of an art gallery down in Truro in Cornwall. We were flown down there in a tiny six-seater plane from Biggin Hill. Stifyn was with me and by total co-incidence we were both wearing white. I had flowing white trousers and a white jacket.

'We look like Steps!' cried Stifyn, as we walked across the tarmac to the plane.

Also on board was the ex-boxer Chris Eubank, who didn't just have a wall of monogrammed Louis Vuitton suitcases, he had a trunk. We were only going for the night!

When we hit cruising altitude, everyone decided it was time for champagne. Stifyn did the honours and the champagne cork shot right across the tiny cabin to hit poor

Chris right in the middle of his forehead. It was not a great moment when you remember that, for all his strange mannerisms, Chris was still a former World Champion.

I drank my champagne fast as we bumped through the clouds and I think I was so nervous about anything else going wrong that I had a second glass. Factor in the altitude and I think I can see why the charity director sitting next to me decided it was time to suggest an even bigger fundraising idea. My companion was Stuart Barber, then celebrity co-ordinator for Breakthrough Breast Cancer.

'Siân, do you fancy doing a sponsored trek across the Himalayas?' he asked.

As I sipped my second glass of champagne, it seemed like a great idea. How hard could it possibly be? I agreed then and there. Fortunately, I have never regretted it for one moment: I was about to find a whole new passion.

There were 22 of us on the Himalayan trek for Breakthrough Breast Cancer in February 2000. I went on my own and shared a tent with the tour leader. Looking back, I still can't believe I went, but I'm so glad I did.

We flew to Kathmandu in Nepal and it looked just the way I hoped it would be: iconic, shallow-roofed temples, mad rickshaws... The rich-brown tones in all the building and the splashes of colour on many of the locals' clothes. Everything appeared resilient and weather-beaten. And little wonder – the weather makes life tough on top of the world, as the 22 of us soon found out.

When we started out, it was gloriously hot on the lower slopes. Ten days later, we were fighting against snow blizzards and biting winds as we tried to get to the summit.

Most of our group fell by the wayside, but seven or eight of us completed the course. It was the experience of a lifetime – with views to match. I had to accept that the Welsh mountains I love so much are mere pimples in comparison.

The people of Nepal were just as wonderful. There seemed to be a lot of music around us, and we played games with the kids in the small villages we passed. At night, our sherpas made incredible vegetable curries and rice dishes, as well as hot, desperately needed sweet tea. Personal hygiene was a matter of a few Wet Wipes: it certainly prepared me for the jungle when *I'm A Celebrity* finally came calling.

My fellow trekkers were a great bunch. We were mostly women but the two or three men in the team had all lost wives to breast cancer. Everyone had stories to tell; everyone had spirit. You don't climb major mountains without a sense of adventure, after all. I was in my element.

'Ingrid, we have to do a trek together.' My old friend Ingrid Tarrant was one of the many people I rushed to talk to when I got back from Nepal. I couldn't stop talking about the experience. Going on that first trip on my own had been far less awkward than I feared. I got on really well with the others and we had all come back as friends. But I knew a group of my own trekking mates would be even better. I researched the market and discovered there are dozens of different charity treks going on around the world. We could raise a lot of money and have some brilliant times.

Back in Britain, I vowed to do more treks as soon as possible. I was fizzing with excitement and I felt I owed it to NCH to support one of its next ventures. Working for

NCH has always grounded me. Its celebrity co-ordinator Vivien Fowle has become a friend, too. Over the years, I have had the chance to visit dozens of the charity's homes in Wales and elsewhere. They open a window on a world many of us might prefer to think didn't exist.

At one of their homes in Penarth near Cardiff, I was told about two new residents, a brother and sister who could hardly speak. Their parents had locked them away in a room for most of their lives. No one ever talked to them, so they never learned to talk themselves. And this was in Cardiff. Those kids had been hidden from sight on the edge of a world city in 20th-century Great Britain! These stories need to be told. On other visits, I see the effects of malnutrition, abuse and criminal neglect.

Fortunately, I also get to witness the good things being done. In Swansea I saw a sense room set up by NCH to help visually impaired children interact with their surroundings and make the most of their lives. There might be chimes, furry toys or perfumed pillows so that the disabled kids can enjoy the senses of touch, smell and hearing. That's the reason why my friends and I all go hiking; why we try to raise as much cash as possible.

One of my other closest friends is David Goldstone. DG and I met at a corporate function in London in 1996 – though the reality isn't quite as glamorous as it sounds. I was hosting a series of breakfasts, lunches and dinners at the BAFTA rooms in London's Piccadilly to promote the revitalised Cardiff Bay. At each session I would introduce the other guests, give a short presentation and then help take questions. We wanted to win as much business for the

Top left: As you can tell, I've been something of a foodie all my life!

Centre left: With brother, David, and sister, Ceri, paying a visit to Santa in the mid-60s.

Above: The young Lloyd siblings celebrate St David's Day in style.

Top right: Ceri, David and I line up with our cousins and our grandfather in his garden. He was such a strong and inspirational figure when I was growing up.

Centre right: I loved London from my first visit. This picture was taken a few years before I discovered Biba on Kensington High Street.

Right: In 1975 the Urdd National Eisteddfod came to Llanelli, and I won the crown for my short stories. This picture made the front page of the *Western Mail*.

Top: The uni gang from Colum Road, and (*inset*) taking a break from all that
studying (and eating!).

Bottom left: Holding my nephew Owen at Ceri and Christian's home in Tours.

Bottom right: I've always been fiercely proud of my country. When I saw an advert in th
Western Mail for a press officer for the Development Board for Rural Wales, I knew th
promoting the region was right up my street.

...e changing – but always smiling – face of Siân Lloyd!

...ockwise from top left: On location for *Wales on Sunday*; my first ever publicity shot; ...the South Bank Studios; and happier and blonder: following my split from Lembit at ...photoshoot for ITV.

© *Media Wales / REX Features*

Top: The weather is at the heart of national life in the UK, and I am fascinated by how climate change is impacting on our lives. I guested on ITV's *This Morning* with Fred Talbot and Michael Fish to discuss the severe conditions our country faces, and (*inset*) with my colleague Becky Mantin.

© *REX Featur*

Above left: It was an incredible accolade to receive the Weather Presenter of the World Award in Paris from Vanessa Paradis, especially since I was chosen by weather presenters from around the world.

Above centre: My weather-presenting skills were put to good use at the Wales Mardi Gras in Cardiff, when I used my friend Stifyn's body as the map, much to the crowd's amusement.

Above right: When I'm not in front of the TV cameras, I do all I can to help promote Wales. Here I am with a couple of our rugby boys. Dewch mlaen fechgyn!

Having a high profile gives me plenty of opportunities to have fun.

Top left: I relished the challenge to attend the premiere of *The Avengers* in fancy dress with my friend Tim Thorne. The skin-tight catsuit (made by LWT's head of wardrobe) went down a storm, and we won the prize for best costume! © *PA Photos*

Top right: My outfit on a *Stars in Their Eyes* special had a touch of glamour – anything to divert the audience's attention from my singing voice. *Inset*: My crazy hat threatened to upstage Jonathan Ross the night we presented the Disney Teacher of the Year awards.
© *REX Features*

Bottom: I went to Paris to learn the can-can from the girls at the Moulin Rouge for an HTV programme. (*Left*) In all our finery as we sailed down the Seine, and (*right*) having a well-earned drink with choreographer Cai Thomas.

I'm a celebrity… get me in there! Being asked to do *I'm a Celeb* was a dream come true for me as I'd never been to Australia and was desperate to go.

Top: With my fellow celebs at the beginning of the series.

Above left: The walk to the camp through the Queensland rainforest was wonderful, as there was so much beautiful flora and fauna to see. At a photoshoot before we flew out, I got a taster of the kind of creatures we'd be rubbing shoulders with.

Above right: I was truly delighted to leave the jungle after two weeks. The OTT Versace Hotel was a splendid setting to catch up with Lembit, whom I had genuinely missed. We spent a fortnight afterwards whizzing around in a little Audi (*inset*). © *REX Featur*

Thanks a bunch !

for sticking with it.

Infuriating, illogical, irritating,

inspiring, irresistible.

Me. x

p left: Lembit and I were a popular couple in his constituency and back in London when
we were out and about. He was unlike any man I'd met and we had some great times
together. However, our views on time-keeping and drinking were utterly incompatible.

© REX Features

p right: A tricky day: from the photoshoot we did in *Hello!* to celebrate
r engagement.

© Lawrence Lawry / Hello!

ttom left: Some honest words in a Valentine's card from Lembit: 'You, Thanks a
unch! for sticking with it. Infuriating, illogical, irritating, inspiring, irresistible, Me x'

ttom right: My Dad, Mum and friend Veronica were hugely supportive when I told
em I had ended things with Lembit. We are pictured on my deck in Wales celebrating
/ parents' golden wedding anniversary.

© Veronica Hollis

Top to bottom: With my good friend David Goldstone at a charity function; Ingrid Tarrant and I having a natter over coffee; in The Ivy with Novello Noades and Hy Money; attending a summer 2007 wedding in my favourite Alice Temperley dress; at a charity football night with GLC's Maggot; and seeing in the millennium with the gorgeous Ioan Gruffudd.

© *Abi Wyles / OK! / Hy Money / REX Featur*

area as possible and showcase it to as many opinion-formers as we could.

I arrived at one of the dinners fresh from a bit of house hunting in North London. Regalian Homes had redeveloped an old warehouse near the canal in Camden. After seeing some adverts, I had my eye on one of the top-floor flats, but, once I had walked around, I decided it was too small and too expensive.

That evening David Goldstone was one of the first people I met after my presentation. I sat next to him at the dinner and asked him what he did for a living. He was the head of Regalian property.

I make up my mind about people pretty quickly and instinctively I knew he was the kind of man who could take a joke. So I told him where I had been that morning and what I had thought. I probably even jokingly asked for a discount. From that moment on, we hit it off. Over the years, we have at some points got together two or three times a week. He is some 30 years older than myself, but we have friends and interests in common and I loved the twinkle that was always in his eye. Together, we go to rugby matches and scream ourselves hoarse. We've had some wonderful singsongs after big games as well. And we've sat on the same tables at countless charity dinners and auctions. We often used to attend events for the Coram Foundation that works with vulnerable children and families around the country, and David was chairman for a number of years. DG and I also share a fascination with politics.

He also used to sit on the board of the Albert Hall, his *alma mater* the London School of Economics, and University College London. I'd often accompany him and his guests to the Albert Hall, where we would sit in the President's Box – we even got to use the royal loo next door!

DG is old Labour, but he was one of the donors who funded Tony Blair's bid for the Labour leadership. He provided office space, furniture, fax machines and telephones. We talk endlessly about the direction of all the parties. His links to LSE have cemented his friendship with Cherie Blair, someone I admired from our first meeting at a Downing Street reception for people who ended up working on Christmas Day such as firemen, nurses and cooks. I've always found her to be a warm and friendly person, a real woman's woman. We met again at a Coram Foundation charity do in Downing Street in 2005 when I was struck by how unaffected she is.

DG has also given me confidence – and advice – in the few low times of my life. He helped me through the legal side of my split with Lembit as I tried to work out what had to be done with the property we had bought. Ultimately, he has been my rock. And that twinkle in his eye means we always laugh when we get together. We are as close as two friends can possibly be.

With so many good friends and so many good things going on in my work, as 2001 got under way, I could hardly complain about life. I was feeling calm, confident and assured; I knew who I was and what I wanted and where I was going. The last thing I needed was some madman turning everything on its head; the last thing I should have done was to get involved with someone like Lembit Opik.

Chapter Eight
Meeting Lembit

I was feeling good the night I first met Lembit Opik. After he complimented me on my shoes, I was feeling even better. What a strange, but surprisingly fascinating man!

My shoes were brand-new Manolo Blahniks with three-inch heels. Every time I wore them, I thought of my favourite *Sex & The City* episode: the one where Carrie takes a wrong turn after lunch and finds herself on one of New York's dangerous side streets and face to face with a mugger.

'Please sir,' she says. 'You can take my Fendi baguette, you can take my ring and my watch but please don't take my Manolo Blahniks.'

I'd bought my pair a while ago and still adored them. Girlfriends loved them as well, but men? Even if they're in to shoes, they don't normally comment on them. Full marks to Mr Lembit Opik – he got my attention right from the start. And things kept getting better.

We met at an engagement party for my old friend

Guto Harri, one of the BBC's most talented political correspondents, in the spring of 2000. I had arrived at Guto's Westminster flat on my own, clutching a bottle of chilled Möet – I remember I was wearing designer jeans and a favourite red Donna Karan top. I was in the mood for a party that night and the whole flat seemed to buzzing with conversation and congratulations.

After giving my best wishes to Guto and his fiancée Shireen, one of the first people I spoke to was Lembit. I don't think I talked to anyone else for the rest of the evening; I don't think I even noticed anyone else.

Guto introduced us and I remember Lembit's big, soft and surprisingly gentle handshake. I also remember noticing how good his skin was – my friend Eileen, who is one of the country's leading beauty experts, is always commenting on people's skin, so I too pay attention to things like that.

As we talked I realised I had seen the man before, very recently. He had been showing off on television. I think it had been *Channel 4 News* that had been doing a profile of up-and-coming politicians. Lembit had been featured, and they filmed him juggling two mobile phones, talking into one and then answering the other when it rang. I suppose the idea was to show just how busy and efficient he could be. Some people might have thought he looked a bit of a fool, but for some reason I found it endearing. He looked like an intelligent man trying to show he understood the modern world. I liked that – I like intelligent men.

I turned up the volume to see the rest of the mini-profile. It turned out the MP was practically a neighbour of mine in Wales. He represented Montgomeryshire, site of many of my old stamping grounds in Newtown. A lot of my old friends would be his constituents and possibly even his voters. Perhaps he should have thought of that before he did the dirty... But that was to come. That first meeting all I could see was Lembit's good side.

Wales featured a great deal in our first conversation that night.

'Have you learned any Welsh?' I asked early on.

'I'm learning,' he said. But then he qualified it: 'I'm *planning* to learn.'

I laughed. It was such a politician's answer. It broke the ice, as if we needed that.

We talked about Newtown to see if we knew people in common and then we had a bit of a debate about Welsh independence. I'm open to it, he's strongly against. And we connected.

Guto's tiny bachelor pad had been filling up all evening and Lembit and I squeezed ever closer in our little corner. Somehow that didn't seem to matter. It was then that he complimented me on my shoes.

'I used to own a shoe shop,' he explained, when I said how unusual it was for him to have noticed them. 'Manolo Blahniks are exquisite,' I said. 'He's personally responsible for the design of every single shoe produced under his name.'

What a charming and surprising man, I thought. How unlikely he would be so into shoes. We laughed and he told me that if I ever came to his house I could have the pick of the leftover stock. Interestingly enough, when I finally got to see them I had to decline the offer. Lembit showed me box after box of high-heeled shoes, my favourite type. But none of them was what you'd call classy, if you know what I mean! I never did get to the bottom of why he still had them around…

We talked – nineteen to the dozen. It seemed we had even more things in common. We started talking about some charity work I had been doing and he said he had recently begun supporting the Spinal Injuries Association.

'I was in a para-gliding accident in the mountains near Plynlimon, in mid-Wales, near Aberhosan.'

'I've walked those mountains.'

'Well, I've crashed into them,' he said. 'I nearly died. The wind just went flat and the chute had deflated into a rag. I headed towards the ground, thinking this is going to do me hard. I dropped 80 feet, fell like a rock. I broke my back in 12 places. Then my ribs, sternum, jaw, and I lost four teeth. The guy I was gliding with thought I was dead.'

I wondered if that explained his slightly twisted, but interesting face.

Lembit talked a little more about the way he was carried to the Royal Shrewsbury Hospital for treatment and then he said something very profound.

'It changes you, almost dying. It makes you realise what's important and what's not. Life's a journey and I'm not too proud to take a lesson from it.'

Lembit was drinking quite a bit that night and for once I think I must have been trying to keep pace and I think I had gone over my usual two glasses of champagne. By now the room was incredibly hot and I suddenly felt light-headed. My head was spinning but I remember thinking this was a man I wanted to see again – but when?

'Do you want to go out for some air?' he asked, noticing me glance over towards the closed windows.

I shook my head. 'I should go home now.' I looked at my watch and got a shock. We had been talking for more than two hours, though it felt like just five minutes.

'I'll come down with you and I'll get you a cab.'

I was inordinately impressed. A man who notices my shoes, a man who sees I'm feeling restless and offers to help me get home – a gentleman! For a moment, I wondered if he might be gay.

Lembit flagged down a black cab straight away. Typical! It was the one time when it might have been nice to be able to stand and wait, talking for a little longer.

'It's been a lovely evening. Thank you,' he said, as he opened the door and stepped aside for me.

I think I was expecting a kiss but there was no hint of one and I'm glad I hadn't leaned forward in hope. Instead, I gave the cab driver my address and sank back into the seat. Then I turned around, looked back through the taxi window and watched Lembit standing under the yellow streetlight. The only thing I hadn't been impressed by was the fabric of his suit – it was shiny, cheap-looking polyester and it looked even worse in the harsh streetlights. But I pushed that thought away as my cab headed north to Camden. It had indeed been a lovely evening, and all the more so for having been so unexpected. Lembit was refreshing, invigorating, intelligent and challenging. If all I had to complain about was a shiny suit, then I was doing pretty well.

Over the next few days and weeks, I'm sure I wondered idly if he might get my number from Guto or Shireen. But then I probably went off and started doing interesting things with Stifyn or Eileen or some of my other friends. I wasn't exactly looking for a new boyfriend and I was incredibly busy at work. So time passed. If I thought about it at all, I felt the shoe-loving Lembit would go down as an opportunity missed. And, when I didn't see him at Guto and Charlie's wedding six months later, I started to forget all about him.

If only I had.

It was a glorious July evening in 2001 when I waved down a taxi outside the London studios to go to ITV's annual 'Politicians Meet the Media' summer party. Having just done the national weather I knew for a fact that we were in for a bright and balmy night. Being a weather forecaster always helps on social occasions like this. I have a head start when it comes to knowing what to wear.

The party was held in Westminster Gardens, pretty much in the shadow of Big Ben. A jazz band was playing, waiters were handing out champagne and canapés, and by the time I arrived there was already a buzz in the air as the guests started to mingle. As usual, it was an eclectic mix – just the way I liked it.

The politicians always seemed to make the effort to attend and the media side of the party was made up of ITV staffers and freelancers, plus a scattering of celebrities and high achievers from all walks of life. I started off the evening chatting to the actress Cherie Lunghi and then had a long discussion with Peter Hain, who would ultimately help me find a really decent man when the toxic Lembit years were finally behind me.

Peter and I had got to know each other during the devolution referendum in Wales in 1997. I was asked to launch the 'Yes' campaign that summer – a huge honour and an issue I believed in wholeheartedly. We worked and socialised together on several other occasions since then.

The band was playing an old Glenn Miller number when the chef, Jean-Christophe Novelli, came over to join my little group. He looked utterly handsome in a crisp, light-blue shirt – and he was completely charming to boot. I told him how much I liked his food and he said he would love me to be a guest at his award-winning Maison Novelli restaurant. It was simple chitchat until he fixed his deep-brown eyes on mine and repeated the invitation.

'It would be an honour for me,' he said, in his sexy French accent. Wow! Could the evening get any better?

'Hello, Siân. I was hoping you would be here.' I had just started talking to *East is East* director Damien O'Donnell when I felt someone touch my arm. It was Lembit. History then started to repeat itself. As we said our hellos, I caught him checking out my shoes.

'Guess the designer this time,' I challenged, with a smile.

But Lembit's mind had already wandered. Now he was looking at my right hand. 'That's a lovely ring,' he remarked.

'Thank you. It's a bespoke Sophie Harley. She's quite a famous jeweller. Do you know of her?'

I was – and still am – very fond of that ring. It was a mix of gold and silver, with Sophie's signature design on the front: a heart with wings on either side.

'It was made specially for me so it fits perfectly,' I said, filling a rare gap in our conversation as Lembit stood looking at it in silence. Little did I know that he already

had plans for that ring. It was about to get me into all sorts
of trouble.

When he snapped out of his reverie Lembit and I carried
on with our conversation. He was being very light-hearted,
semi-flirtatious and very frothy that night. I loved it – and
the magic was far from over.

As we talked, a small man with white hair and a
pinstriped suit came up to greet Lembit – I would soon
discover that people were always coming over to greet
Lembit in Parliament. This man was holding one of the
huge umbrellas ITV had brought along in case of rain.
They really should have asked me first if we might need
them – I could have saved them a lot of money!

'Would everyone like to top off the evening with a little
tour of the Gallery?' the man asked our group.

He didn't even wait for a reply. Instead, he simply
marched off ahead, pointing out various gargoyles, statues
and towers with his umbrella as we followed in his wake.
It was a cross between the Pied Piper of Hamelin and the
Grand Old Duke of York. I loved the impromptu tour
because it focused on the House of Lords of which I knew
far less than the House of Commons. The tour finished
when our guide swung the umbrella around in a circle,
hooked it under his left arm and wished us all a very
cordial goodnight. It really was like some sort of magical
film. We all looked at each other, unsure whether or not to
laugh. It had been a strange and special evening. No one
seemed to want it to end – and Jean-Christophe decided it
didn't have to.

'Come to my place now and I'll cook for you all,' he said.

MEETING LEMBIT

It would have been rude to refuse.

We all walked out past the police guards into Parliament Square. Big Ben had long since struck midnight but there was still plenty of traffic passing Winston Churchill's statue on the green. As we looked up at the sky, Lembit began a whole new conversation.

'It's not a matter of if, it's a matter of when,' he said, a propos pretty much nothing.

'What?' I asked.

'The asteroid.'

'Lembit, what are you talking about?'

This was the most ridiculous conversation I had ever heard. Who, apart from nerdy schoolboys, talked about asteroids? Silly as it seemed, it seemed utterly right and endearing that Lembit would start a conversation about them. He appeared to be a gawky little boy in a gangly man's body. I thought it was lovely. And he wasn't letting the subject go.

'It's a fact,' he said. 'Scientists agree the chances of an asteroid having an impact that could wipe out most of the human race is 100 per cent. We should be extremely worried. It's time to sit up and take notice.'

Quite possibly this was when he had me. All my life I have loved men and women with passions. I come from campaigning stock and I thrive when I've got a cause to support. Lembit's asteroid impacts might seem a little offbeat, but the subject came from his heart and I was drawn to it.

Our group managed to flag down two cabs immediately – it really was a charmed night – and soon we were on our way to Jean-Christophe's restaurant in Clerkenwell.

But, as far as dear Lembit was concerned, danger was all around.

'We need an all-party task force to assess the potentially catastrophic risk posed by orbiting rocks,' he declared, refusing to let his pet subject drop.

With very little traffic on the streets, it took us next to no time to get to Maison Novelli. The waiters had just finished cleaning up and looked a little worried to see their boss come back through the door. But Jean-Christophe just waved his arms in the air and sent them all home. We would be looked after by the man himself – this was his night. What an extraordinary privilege!

Lembit sat on my right on a large circular table lit by a single spotlight on the ceiling. Certainly he had stamina. He started to tell a series of stories about Parliament – they were hilarious and the whole table almost in tears of laughter. Who knew he could be so amusing? He seemed the perfect addition to any dinner party.

The jokes helped the time fly and soon Jean-Christophe came out of the kitchen carrying big plates of freshly prepared antipasto. There was cured ham, marinated vegetables, olives, pepperoni, provolone and fresh mozzarella. More bottles of wine and champagne suddenly appeared on the table and we all started to tuck in as Lembit proposed a toast.

'We should all eat, drink and be merry...' he began.

'Because tomorrow we could all be hit by an asteroid,' I interrupted.

Everyone laughed, and I noticed Lembit laughed loudest of all. It felt good to be able to finish his sentence like this and get a good reaction. Obviously, I had been gently making fun of him but he hadn't minded. That was a great sign. It felt as if we had connected. And I think he felt it too.

It meant I was smiling broadly when Jean-Christophe arrived with our main course. It was steak – the best steak I have ever tasted. Pinky-red in the centre and so tender it really did melt in the mouth. At the end of the night, Jean-Christophe handed us all a copy of his latest cookbook. I cherish it to this day as a keepsake of a very special evening and a source of some wonderful recipes. So, once again Jean-Christophe, I'm sorry for that night on *Hell's Kitchen* all those years later in 2006 when I picked Gary Rhodes's food over your menu.

On that one particular evening I just felt like trying some of Gary's food for a change. And it was fun to be with a group of pals who could dub themselves 'Gary's girls' for the night. But, trust me, I've never forgotten that night in Maison Novelli. And I do still use your cookbook.

Back in 2001, two other events spring to my mind. The first was the way Lembit looked. The light did us all favours that night – how I love good lighting. It made Lembit's skin look even better and it picked out a real sparkle in his eyes. He cracked jokes and was the life and soul of our party into the small hours. And there was an edge to him that I don't think many people ever get to see.

It seems a strange thing to say about a Member of Parliament, but I spotted a wild and reckless side to Lembit. It was a side that really appealed to me – it was a time in my life when I wanted to go with the flow. Believe it or not, Lembit seemed like a bad boy that night. And bad boys can sometimes be very attractive indeed.

The second thing I remember was the moment when his hand brushed mine under the table. It was unexpected and just a little too soon in company, I thought. I moved my hand away. Then Lembit said something odd: 'It was just a trick,' he said enigmatically, failing to explain what he had been doing.

The following morning I realised what this trick had been. Somehow Lembit had managed to take my Sophie Harley ring off my finger. He had done it in the middle of a meal, surrounded by other people and without my noticing a thing. I probably should have been annoyed or at least concerned. Instead, I was ever so slightly thrilled. I hoped this strange man would carry on surprising me for some time yet, though in the meantime my first priority was just to get my favourite ring back.

'I took it to make sure I would see you again,' he told me over the phone when I tracked him down.

'Well, look after it,' I told him. 'It means a lot to me.'

We arranged a time and place to meet up, but Lembit had to cancel at the last moment because of some crisis in the House. I was going through a hugely busy patch at work as well so it was nearly a month before we could arrange to meet again. But this time he had another reason for staying away.

'What do you mean, you can't find it?' I was trying to keep things light, but this time I was fed up.

Lembit's magician act no longer seemed so endearing. If he had wanted to see me again, why wasn't he man enough to ask me out on a date? Why the song and dance of stealing something that was really precious to me?

And what kind of man would then lose his prospective girlfriend's ring?

With hindsight, it should have been a sign that life with Lembit was always going to be full of surprises – and that not all of them would be good.

For a host of reasons the months raced away before I saw Lembit again. It sounds silly, but I didn't want to meet up until he had grown up and found my ring. And that took nearly a year.

Ffion Hague was a friend of mine well before the summer of 2002. We had met through our Social Welsh and Sexy society. Her sister Manon was also a member and a big supporter. She was with me when I finally set up my next date with Lembit. We had just left George's, a private dining club in Mayfair, after a lively catch-up over lunch. I turned on my phone and had two messages: the first was from the BBC confirming that I had two tickets to the Proms at the Royal Albert Hall. The second was from Lembit. He had found my ring – behind the seat of his MG, apparently – and wanted to meet so that he could finally return it to me.

After saying goodbye to Ffion, I called him.

'If you give me my ring back, I'll invite you to the Proms,' I said.

It was a date.

We met in the main entrance and I took the ring straight away and slipped it back on my finger. Bearing in mind the ridiculous amount of fuss this had caused, I was feeling a little cooler towards my companion that night. And I was immediately reminded of how awful his clothes were. Once more, his suit was shiny and ugly. His tie was just as bad. I wanted to burn them both.

But as we grabbed a drink in the bar our conversation pushed these thoughts aside. Lembit was at his most charming. We talked about politics and current events and Wales – three of my favourite subjects. They say the brain is the sexiest organ in the body. As we took our seats and waited for the concert to begin, I was ready to agree. Once it did we were both carried away by the music, though I kept my hands firmly clasped in the middle of my lap – Lembit was not to try any more tricks.

Our conversation became personal and more serious after we left the Albert Hall and walked out into Kensington Gore. I gave Lembit a lift to the tube station but instead of him leaping out of the car we sat and talked for ages, in Cavendish Square of all places! First of all we talked about alcoholism – hardly the most romantic of subjects, but somehow it cropped up as we discussed various people in the public eye. He claimed it was a subject close to his heart for personal reasons, but I didn't feel it was appropriate to ask him why.

Then Lembit surprised me yet again.

It was a clear night and even with all the streetlights of London it was just about possible to see stars in the sky. Lembit clearly knew them well.

'Do you see that one there?' he asked, pointing out one of the brightest. 'Now look to the left of it. Then between that star and the one to its left, can you see a very faint one?'

He told me this final star was his favourite. Also, that there was an asteroid named after his grandfather Ernst Opik, a famous astronomer back in Estonia. Who would have thought that less than six months later we would be doing a programme on said Ernst Opik out in the university town of Tartu in Estonia!

When Lembit finally got out of the car and headed for the tube, I thought he might kiss me. But once again he didn't try and this in itself seemed intriguing. I do want to see you again, I thought, as he disappeared into the Underground – and not just to help you buy a better suit.

Chapter Nine

First Dates

O ur first proper date was at the Red Lion pub on
Parliament Street in Whitehall. It is the closest pub
to Downing Street and is used by so many MPs and political
reporters that the televisions show BBC's Parliament
Channel instead of the usual Sky Sports.

It was 11 September 2002, the first anniversary of the
terrorist attacks in America. No one in the pub seemed to
mention this all evening, which I thought strange, though
memories of what had gone before did keep flitting in and
out of my mind.

Despite the inauspicious date and air of nervousness in
London, the Red Lion was bursting at the seams when I
arrived. Inappropriate as it seemed, there appeared to be
some sort of celebration going on – and Lembit was at the
centre of it. He was joint chairman of the Middle Way
group and had just finished a debate about fox hunting

that had gone particularly well for him. Politicians from all sides, from Sinn Fein to the Conservatives, crowded round him. The women, in particular, seemed to be hanging on to his every word. Interesting... I was surprised one or two of them were less than warm and welcoming towards me.

When he saw me, Lembit broke away from his group and welcomed me with a big smile and a kiss. I said hello to all his colleagues, noticing that one of the female researchers scowled rather than smiled as I was introduced. I will certainly have to watch out for you, I thought.

'Nice shoes,' he said. 'It's my round. Have you got a note you could lend me?' I laughed at Lembit's disorganised nature. What kind of idiot would come out with no cash and have to borrow from a potential new girlfriend? If he was trying to impress me, then clearly he was playing it very cool indeed. But maybe I liked that. Besides, he was a terribly busy man, wasn't he? And, in any case, surely he'd pay me back?

I handed him £20 and asked for a white wine. When Lembit came back with a tray of drinks, he suggested we try to find a table outside.

We all talked for an hour or so and I noticed a group of young researchers seemed particularly keen to get close to Lembit. I handed over another £20 note so we could buy another round, though I was starting to wonder when all these hangers-on were going to pick up their laptop bags and leave. I hadn't gone on a lot of first dates in my life, but even I knew this one was a little unusual. Especially as one particular woman – the scowler – seemed glued to her spot. She made a lot of eye contact with Lembit, touched his leg when they talked and clearly knew him well.

But I outlasted her. When she and the rest of the group all finally left Lembit and I on our own, I felt like cheering. But as Lembit seemed to know so many other people in the pub I felt I had to get us away before we were waylaid again. I am a member of Soho House in Greek Street. It would be just the place for us.

'Let's go there for a nightcap,' I suggested.

We held hands as we walked up towards Trafalgar Square and on into Soho. Lembit had drunk quite a lot at that point so he swayed in and out of the street and I kept guiding him back on to the pavements. It reminded me of student days, though when I'd actually been a student I had mostly acted like a middle-aged woman! Strange, how life works out.

I signed Lembit into the club and we headed up to the bar on the top floor. There are some comfy sofas and quiet corners up there and we sat close and talked and talked and talked. Lembit had what felt like a hundred stories to tell about Estonia and astronomy; I probably had a hundred more about Wales and the weather. I drank sparkling water, laughed and listened a lot. Lembit also talked about his ambitions. Clearly, he saw himself as potential Lib Dem leadership material. Back then, I didn't know any differently so it seemed intoxicating.

When we left Soho House in the early hours, we both knew what was going to happen. We got into a taxi and headed back to my top-floor flat in Camden. That night neither of us got much sleep!

Luckily for me, I could have a bit of a lie-in the next morning – I wasn't working until the afternoon. But Lembit was up at 7.30 for meetings. He picked his suit up off the floor, where it had lain in a crumpled heap all night.

As he left and I drifted back to sleep, I had three key thoughts in my mind.

First, that it was incredible that he could do a full day's work after just a couple of hours' sleep and had no hangover. Second, that if were going to start dating seriously I would have to take him shopping for a better suit. Third, that he would have to learn to use a coat hanger.

So, what else attracted me to this strange and unlikely man? I think I liked the fact that he clearly had flaws and deficiencies – I think women can be great fixers of men, that we see the diamond in the lump of coal. We want to unearth and polish it. In Lembit I saw someone who clearly needed fixing and I was up for the challenge. I was convinced I could change him for the better, that I would be able to calm him down and soften his rough edges. I also thought his wild side might be good for me too. Maybe I had always played my love life too safe. Perhaps I had always been too steady in my relationships. Right through my twenties, I had lived a middle-aged life with Mark and it had been good to feel like a teenager again. Perhaps it was time I rebelled and had some more fun. Lembit and I would be good for each other, I thought, as I fell back into sleep that long, lazy morning.

We saw each other almost every day from then on, and he turned out to be a surprisingly romantic man.

One moonlit evening Lembit went down on to his knees and serenaded me with 'Fly Me To The Moon' on the balcony of my flat. Another time I got a Dean Martin classic in the street. Sometimes we wrapped up warmly in the autumn air and sat on my balcony, looking out over the rooftops and lights of North London. Other evenings we played chess and scrabble late into the night. Or Lembit would pick up takeaways from Wagamamas in Camden and we would eat them in bed watching classic films. It was simple, relaxed stuff; it was wonderful. Lembit claimed this was the happiest he had ever been in his life and that at last he knew the meaning of true love. I loved him saying that.

The more I learned about him, the more fun he seemed. He had joined some bizarre band, recorded a single and tried to get the song in the charts. It didn't make it, but how many other MPs would have had the nerve to do something like that? He was so much better-looking and so much less geeky in real life than on television. I loved introducing him to my friends because I knew he would always exceed their expectations. The first night he met my friends Trish and Eric in a tapas bar in Camden he was late and quite tipsy, but he was on superb form when he finally showed up. He told some great stories, fired off jokes and was utterly compulsive. I was thrilled that this wild, jocular man was with me.

Best of all, our passions and pastimes seemed to gel as well. We were both lifelong film fans and, when I was in London, I loved getting a text from Lembit: 'Just having a quick social, will be back at 9.30 for the late showing'.

I would meet him outside Parliament or near our flat in Camden. Together we would walk hand in hand to the nearest cinema, normally stopping along the way to buy a couple of small bottles of wine to sneak in as a treat for Lembit. As the lights went down Lembit would link his leg around mine and we would slip back down in our seats. Often around 20 minutes into the movie, I would feel his leg relax its grip. When I looked over, he would be asleep. I smiled. It was cosy, companionable and endearing. All I had to do was grab the empty wine bottle from his hand so it didn't smash on the floor and get us thrown out. And I didn't mind that he hardly ever saw the films all the way through. I found it strangely appealing that he was so busy, and so tired. I was always happy to tell him what he had missed.

After a month I gave Lembit a key to my flat. Then, after three months, he moved in with me. He was then able to let a friend stay in his flat near Parliament and I was pleased to be able to look after him a bit more.

Fairly early on I got in the first of my many shopping trips. I still shudder at the thought of the shiny suit he was wearing at our first meeting at Guto Harri's party. At ITV's summer party in Westminster Gardens and our first few dates at the Proms and in Whitehall I soon realised this wasn't a one-off. Lembit might be an unusual Lib Dem member in many ways, but he was spot-on in the fashion stakes. They have to be the worst-dressed party in the country! I'll never forget the shock of seeing them all together at conference one time and thinking, What a bunch of odds and sods! Lembit might be a little colour blind, but that was no excuse for some of the food stains on his ties and trousers.

It made me laugh that, for all the sheep farmers in his constituency, Lembit was something of a stranger to wool and other natural fibres. And, while he might have been able to argue that 'wipe-clean polyester' was a practical choice, he didn't seem to avail of its dubious advantages.

Food and drink stains didn't ever get wiped off; nothing seemed to get cleaned.

So Lembit's wardrobe was my first big project. I enjoyed the challenge. His shiny, reflective suits went to Oxfam. Instead, I helped him choose alternatives more suitable for a man who felt he could go right to the top. I suggested the likes of YSL and Paul Smith for big occasions and, for everyday wear, I found quality basics from Ted Baker and M&S. And I helped pick matching shirts and some bold modern ties. I paid for them because the new look had been my idea. And as the months rolled on I took charge of their dry cleaning as well. I don't think that was something Lembit would ever have thought of doing on his own.

The biggest buzz I got out of Lembit in those first few months came from his job. I had always loved spending time with politicians. Activism was in my blood, from my grandfather in the National Union of Mineworkers to my mother and the National Union of Teachers All the arguments round our kitchen table about everything from nuclear power to communism. I was the girl brought up to debate topical issues. Who better to debate them with than someone who makes his living in the mother of all Parliaments?

Being with Lembit fitted in perfectly with so many other parts of my life. There was my acquaintance with the likes of Peter Hain, Dafydd Wigley and the Hagues and with people such as Huw Edwards and Guto Harri as well as heavyweight politically aware friends like David Goldstone. It also made me feel as if I had slipped back into the good old days in Elgin Crescent when Karl and I waited up to hear the latest House of Commons' gossip from Kim Howells.

All this had always pointed towards my becoming the perfect politician's partner. Lembit was in the prewritten script of my life. Sometimes it felt as if I had no choice in the matter – and for a long time I didn't want one either. In those early days, everything about this tall odd-looking man seemed right. Even his strange hobbyhorses were fascinating to me.

We talked more about astronomy and all the things his grandfather Ernst Opik had taught him about the stars and the solar system. It was seriously intellectual stuff and I devoured it. My old sensitivities about having too much of an arts-based education meant I was always ready to immerse myself in anything scientific. In Lembit, I had a great new teacher. We sparked each other off. My meteorology was a perfect match for his astronomy. We couldn't stop talking.

The next big thrill of being with Lembit was also connected to the skies.

'I fly planes,' he told me in one of our earliest conversations when we talked about our interests.

As hobbies go, you don't get much more impressive than that.

In our first few months as a couple, he offered to take me up for a ride. The first plane he rented that day was a pretty rickety old thing. But I always felt safe with Lembit: he never took chances in the air; he never drank if he was flying the next day. And it was so much fun. I loved seeing him in his helmet and gloves, excited and ready for the off.

I was also happy to help out. My forecasting skills meant I was the ideal co-pilot. I sat next to him in the cockpit, with the clipboard carrying all our vital flight information and a felt-tip pen to mark up any changes. I enjoyed researching our routes and trying to master the technical details of each plane. Flying involved teamwork and Lembit and I were perfectly in tune with each other.

Our flights could also be thrilling and exhilarating. RAF jets would sometimes shoot past us. As we pierced through the clouds, we saw the most wonderful views. We would scream out jokes and laugh as we gazed down on the Welsh countryside. Flying made us both feel alive. I also loved the tiny airports we used. The landing strip at Welshpool Airport is like something out of an old movie or period drama. There are hills all around and sheep graze just past the tarmac.

As a private pilot, Lembit had to clock up a lot of hours in the air to retain his licences. He was also doing meteorological exams and training in night flying. The fast learner in me enjoyed the challenge of reading the set texts alongside him and testing him for his exams. We learned together, sharing something important and exciting. As far as Lembit was concerned, the only problem with the planes was their vast cost. Renting them was far from cheap and he never seemed to have any spare cash. After a while, he became part of a syndicate of owners but I never got the impression that this made things much cheaper. I was happy to subsidise Lembit's other spending, though his inability to keep on top of his finances was a concern. It was a constant surprise to me that his bank allowed him to get more and more overdrawn. I tried so hard to get him to be sensible and responsible about money, but he refused to discuss it in any way. He once missed a mortgage payment and even then refused to discuss his finances! Like everything else in his life, Lembit genuinely did not think he was answerable to me or anyone else. My argument that flying a private plane was a luxury he couldn't afford fell on deaf ears. Lembit claimed it was like an addiction, and that he *had* to fly.

I do like people who are passionate about their hobbies. I'm impressed by people who make financial or other sacrifices because they have other interests to pursue so, if that meant me paying for all our meals or other travel, that was a deal worth making. And for a while I got some great fringe benefits. If we were flying, we could get to my old friend Eileen in Cornwall in little more than an hour – it would have taken at least four times as long by road. So I was able to see so much more of her.

Because friends mean the world to me, it was so important that Lembit fitted in. And he did, at least at first. Funnily enough, he got in Eileen's good books the same way he had got into mine. The first time they met, he complimented her on her shoes. Maybe it was just an old line he used, but back then it did the trick.

Back on the ground, for me the icing on the cake was that dating Lembit took me back to Newtown, where I had lived so happily as a press officer for the Development Board for Rural Wales. I still had so many friends there. Now I had a reason to spend even more time with Veronica and her husband John and all the others.

Whenever I was in the constituency, I felt as if I was coming home. I knew little places, cafes, restaurants and local pubs that Lembit didn't; I had networks of friends he could tap into. At a charity auction we held in the constituency, I felt utterly at home. The whole room was full of friendly faces from my past – and hopefully my future. I got caught up in all the fun and enthusiasm, and bid £50 for one of Huw Edwards's silk ties – even though Huw is an old pal who would have given it to me for free! Being able to pass it on to Lembit raised a lot of laughs and made our evening even more memorable.

The final test in Wales was for Lembit to meet my parents. I knew that, even if they hated him, they wouldn't dream of saying anything. They support all their children in everything we do and they rely on the grounding they have given us to see us through any disasters in the end. And I don't think they thought Lembit was a disaster – at least not then.

They clearly felt he was eclectic, quirky and unconventional. He was a free thinker, an original. So, even if a few warning bells did go off, they gave us their silent blessing. To the outside world at least, Lembit was everything I was looking for in a man.

And it's not as if I didn't have plenty of other good examples to learn from. It had been pretty much love at first sight for Ceri and Christian all those years ago in France. Their relationship has gone from strength to strength ever since. And they're not the only ones to have found soul mates in the blink of an eye: my childhood friend Novello has been married to Ron Noades for over 25 years.

Novello went on a training course for a part-time job she had during the first summer holidays of her university years. She was put up in a hotel in Bristol, where one of the other guests was football boss Ron Noades, who was scouting out players for Crystal Palace. She bumped into him in the hotel bar and he fell in love with her smiling eyes. He asked her to marry him the following day. They are still the most wonderful couple and firm inspirational friends. Then there is my weather colleague and dear friend Robin MacCallum. He married his wife Siobhan within three months of meeting her and they are one of the happiest couples you would ever wish to meet.

'When you know, you know,' Carole Smillie once told me in the make-up room at Yorkshire Television.

So did I know about Lembit? I certainly hadn't fallen in love with him at first sight. He had intrigued me, but it had taken a long time for anything to develop. Now that it had, I think I had fallen into a trap that lies before a lot of otherwise sensible women. I hadn't fallen in love with the real Lembit, instead I had fallen in love with the idea of who he might *become*. And I was convinced I could help him along the way.

Chapter Ten

The Politician's 'Wife'

Going on the road with Lembit triggered the start of a whole new political adventure. Every ambitious MP must pay their dues to their party so Lembit had to travel the length and breadth of the country, going from town to town and function to function to meet the party faithful. He had to shine – he had to press the flesh and woo all the grass-roots supporters and local activists.

These are the people who ultimately choose the next party president. Lembit wanted this to be him. He also felt that one day he could be party leader as well, even Prime Minister. And I was impressed with his enthusiasm. Even though I wasn't a party supporter, I would support *him* as much as possible.

Night after night, I would meet Lembit in Newtown or London and drive for hours while he slept in the passenger seat. Our meetings could be anywhere from the Southwest to East Anglia to the Northeast. Sometimes we were on the road for four hours at a time. I drove in all weathers and didn't even mind that with Lembit asleep I only had the radio as company. Not bad commitment from someone who didn't even support or vote for the Lib Dems!

When we found the meeting halls we would sometimes have to get changed in the car park before walking into the venue. But then the magic began…

Lembit was a master at putting on a show. He was a charmer and could go from comatose wreck to sparkling raconteur in minutes. Often I would watch in amazement as he worked the room. If only those people laughing at his jokes could have seen him less than 30 minutes earlier.

From the start I got plenty of approving nods, smiles and comments from people in London and his constituency. They could see that my 'new and improved' Lembit was looking smarter. We were a winning team. With a steady girlfriend on his arm, at last he had an air of respectability. At the very least he was dressed for success. He really did seem to have changed.

'He has certainly changed for the better since meeting you,' one of the lovely older ladies in his constituency told me after a meeting. I was happy to help do even more.

Right from the start, I was surprised to discover there were big gaps in Lembit's knowledge of Wales. He didn't understand that Wales was different and he wasn't terribly interested in the people or institutions, or the Assembly. Not only this, but he was constantly trying to mimic the mid-Wales accent. But I was ready to try to educate him and fill in the blanks. My family background and my interest in Welsh affairs meant I was ideally placed to tell him what mattered and why. I urged him to read the *Western Mail* and the *Daily Post* to get a feel for things.

But wasn't Lembit just a little bit odd? I think I was aware right from the start that a lot of people didn't really get him – they found his looks and his intensity, along with his odd sense of humour, a bit disturbing. But that only made me keener. I have always had a strange respect for mavericks and genuine originals. In a funny sort of way, I think Prince Charles was a perfect example. He was always being mocked for his thoughts on everything from the environment to architecture but, having met him, I knew how deeply he thought about these issues. I knew that his charity, The Prince's Trust, did an incredible amount of important work but was often overlooked. The Prince ignored the critics and kept plugging away at his cause, something I respected.

And I felt that in our own minor way Lembit and I could do similar good in his constituency and beyond. He was one of the few early voices to demand action over the series of unexplained 'suicides' at the Deepcut Army Barracks. Where many would have given up, he plugged away at the cause long afterwards. In mid-Wales, I loved Lembit's enthusiasm and passion. He never shirked his local surgeries or shied away from voters. When he met people in his offices or in the street, he seemed able, articulate and determined to help.

And people did depend upon him. They relied on the levers he could pull, the changes he could make. It was impressive, admirable stuff, and it dazzled me.

In our first months and years together, Lembit also impressed me with the way he dealt with other people. He would never speak badly of anyone; he was never critical behind their backs. In social terms, he was the ultimate democrat. He would no more condemn a person for taking drugs than he would for having an extramarital affair. Never judgemental, he saw everyone as equals. By now, I had been immersed in the sometimes bitchy, backstabbing world of television for some 20 years. For me, Lembit was a breath of pure fresh air.

Of course, not everything can always be perfect in a relationship. And from the very start two things looked set to be problems with Lembit and me. The first was punctuality, the second alcohol.

As a broadcaster, timing matters to me. Doing live reports makes you conscious of every passing second. But I soon realised that Lembit can ignore whole hours. In the early days of our relationship, he was late for almost every date we had. For a while, that was all part of his appeal. He was like a mad professor, too busy to be bothered by inconveniences like the ticking of the clock – and somehow he always managed to get away with it.

I remember the time he was due on Radio 4's *Any Questions* – a gig he had been thrilled to do.

I had the radio on in my car as I headed back to Wales. Jonathan Dimbleby went through all the standard introductions to panel members, who said their usual hellos and got polite applause from the audience.

But where was Lembit?

'And in a moment I can introduce you to MP Lembit Opik because he has only just arrived,' David said, to my mind not sounding entirely pleased.

I laughed out loud in my car. Only Lembit could be late

for a live radio show! I knew I would have to take charge next time and ensure he had left enough time for his journey. And I was happy to. Because, however put out I was at waiting for him of an evening, we never had a dull moment once he finally arrived.

I forgave a lot of the lateness because I genuinely thought MPs were terribly busy due to their workload. I'd heard that people like Simon Hughes, for instance, were always very late for everything. To be fair to Lembit, there was a stage during which he really did try to be vaguely on time for things. Sometimes he managed to be only 15 minutes or so late, which he regarded as a triumph and insisted on being praised for. He would repeatedly ask, 'Are you pleased? Are you pleased?' punctuated by, 'Do you love me? Do you love me? Tell me you love me.' It was like being with a precocious child.

The alcohol situation would be harder to resolve. At first, it wasn't about what Lembit himself consumed, more about the people around him. In the early months of our relationship, the politico in me was in my element in Westminster. It was a huge privilege to have such easy access to Parliament through my boyfriend. The terrace bar on the banks of the Thames has to be one of the most beautiful places in London for a drink. Being able to eat in the dining rooms inside the House of Commons and the new Portcullis House is just as exciting. Lembit was extremely popular in the bars and dining rooms and at first I enjoyed being shown off there. I liked that he wanted me to meet his colleagues and his sparring. Partners – not least because I liked sparring along with them all as well. But Parliament's heavy-drinking culture soon wore me down. They seemed to take pride in how much they drank.

The bars were beautiful – it was just such a shame about some of the people. The amount of alcohol MPs of all parties consumed blew my mind. And after a while I noticed what was really going on. I could tell that the political heavyweights were never propping up Annie's Bar or the Strangers' Bar. The serious politicians just popped in to each place to do their business and then made their excuses. It was usually the failures, the old soaks, the also-rans and the no-hopers that took advantage of those ridiculously cheap, subsidised bar tariffs. It was usually the same, prematurely old, always slurring people. The ruddy faces, the loud voices, then there were the ambitious researcher types who didn't have a life outside Westminster and would sell their own mothers to get on in the party.

I had hoped to have inspiring, uplifting conversations in the Westminster bars. Instead, I heard the same sexist comments and the same old jokes and endless anecdotes. And these are the people who write our laws! I was horrified to think that, at the time, those people were drawing up new legislation on extended opening hours. Lembit used to accuse me of having a problem with drink. I would always patiently try to point out to him that, no, I didn't have a problem with drink; I had a problem with *heavy* drinking, that I thought it destroyed people and relationships. In time, it would play a huge part in destroying mine.

Lembit told me he loved me within a couple of weeks of us dating. And from then on he told me all the time. Some evenings he would just repeat it. 'I love you, I love you, I love you, I love you,' what felt like a hundred times. So I told him I loved him too – it would have been rude not to!

But had the words just been dragged out of me? I wasn't exactly infatuated with him, but I was dazzled and inspired by him. But, like I say, I think I was still keener on the man I knew he could be. In the early days, I was more in love with his potential. I firmly believed he would calm down, grow up and become a person of substance.

'You mark my words, I'll end up at Number Ten,' he once told me.

It's laughable now, but he managed to make it sound less so back then. I think all I did was smile wryly. 'Not in the Lib Dems, you won't, matey!' I wanted to say.

On a better note I did appreciate that Lembit was changing for me. I soon got fed up with being shown off in the House of Commons bars and for a while he started to come home earlier so we could spend more time together. We saw more films, enjoyed lots of lovely, home-cooked food and more evenings in my flat. The wild party animal in Lembit seemed to have been tamed. We were living our lives on an even keel and it felt great, so we both knew it was time to put down some proper roots.

Lembit owned a townhouse in the centre of Newtown. When we were feeling kind, my friends and I used to call it 'the student house'. And, when we were being more honest, we named it 'the hovel'.

I knew it desperately needed a woman's touch. In truth, it would have taken a team of industrial cleaners to make it habitable – a microbiologist could have been employed for a week on the contents of the fridge alone! And I don't think the toilet had ever been cleaned before I arrived on the scene. Lembit used to love telling people that he knew I must be in love with him when he arrived home one day to find me on my hands and knees in rubber gloves cleaning his loo!

Of course, Lembit never got round to hiring those industrial cleaners and he prevented me from doing so. He had Quentin Crisp's attitude to dirt and grime – you don't notice it after the first couple of years. And he saw no reason to think anyone else would notice either. I cringed with embarrassment that he had people like Simon Hughes and other MPs to stay, sleeping in damp rooms in un-made-up beds with crumpled sheets.

It was clear we needed a fresh start together. So, as we eased into the second year of our relationship, we went house hunting out in the mid-Wales countryside. For a while, nothing really grabbed us. Then we found our place in a village on the outskirts of Newtown. The house wasn't in great shape and would need a lot of work to turn it into a dream home, but its rooms were perfectly proportioned, its position gave it the most incredible views and, like Lembit, I knew it had fantastic potential.

'This is it,' he said, as we walked around.

'It's great,' I agreed, already imagining us there. 'We *have* to get it!'

So we did. We bought it together and started our new life in the middle of the stunning hills. Although we had been right about the amount of work the house needed, like most people we actually underestimated the size of the job. But I was happy to make time for it. The homemaker in me rushed to the fore. I spent ages choosing the best furniture and I splashed out on some wonderful Celtic art. My fellow SWS member Laurence Llewelyn-Bowen would have been proud of me. Our makeover was better than anything you might see on television: it was the one house where I never really skimped on anything. I spent whatever it took to make everything perfect – and it was.

With homes to share in London and the country, Lembit and I felt utterly established as a couple. Our relationship had taken a long time to get off the ground, but now we were fully committed. I truly felt it could be for keeps. Now, when he told me he loved me, I could reply wholeheartedly and without a single reservation. I was happy.

Being in the middle of rural Wales brought another benefit. It meant Lembit had to drink less. Just like many other politicians, and indeed other people in positions of high stress who work long hours such as journalists and barristers, the culture of doing business in bars and attending countless evening functions meant that drinking was unavoidably part of his life. Alcohol has long been the curse of politicians: after all, Winston's Churchill's fondness for a drink with his cigar was well documented. Lembit was scrupulous about never drinking and driving, so his liver probably got a bit of a rest now he had to travel home by car. His bank balance must have looked a tad healthier, too, though he still didn't usually have any cash – his card was forever being refused at ATM machines, he said.

From midnight on a Saturday to midnight on a Sunday, Lembit would not drink any alcohol at all. This no alcohol on a Sunday rule allowed him to claim that it proved he didn't have a problem with drink. The reality of the situation was that he often drank shots of shorts in the minutes leading up to midnight on a Saturday, and would then uncork a bottle of red wine come midnight on a Sunday night. I witnessed this scenario so many times. Two examples spring to mind – once at the Hilton Hotel in Cardiff he knocked back three shots of whisky, one after the other, in about ten minutes. The other was the fiftieth birthday of his PA in the constituency office. Again, as the clock ticked down to midnight, he threw those shots down his throat...

Nevertheless, and when alcohol was not in the equation, I felt as though we were doing the right thing. It was a warm spring day shortly after we had settled in when Lembit walked around, almost as if seeing the place for the first time.

'This is perfect, just perfect,' he told me. 'I love you more than anyone. You're the best thing that has ever happened to me. I love you, I love you, I love you,' he repeated.

I held his hand and smiled. We were a great team and I knew we would thrive in mid-Wales. Everything was looking good – well, nearly everything.

Chapter Eleven
Storm Clouds

Can you judge someone by the company they keep? Of course you can. And in the back of my mind I was becoming increasingly wary of Lembit's two friends: the former DJ Andy Kershaw and one of his old mates in the constituency, David Hamer.

I first met Andy a year or so after Lembit and I started dating. Back in 2001, I had agreed to go to a Lib Dem ball as Lembit's guest and, of course, when the time came, it turned out to be hugely inconvenient. But I'd given my word and so I decided to attend the ball and drive down the M4 to Cardiff straight afterwards.

Andy was with us on the top table and the drink was clearly flowing. I felt that this was a man who liked his drink, but couldn't really handle it. That night in the Grosvenor, he was very aggressive and I felt embarrassed for Lembit as the host of our table. I think what bothers me when people get drunk is their unpredictability. Maybe it's because I forecast things for a living – I like to know what's going to happen next.

When alcohol takes hold of someone, I can't rely on my instinct any more. The nicest people can turn aggressive and violent; the most charming become silent and morose. And I never know what I'm supposed to do to calm them down or cheer them up.

The second time I met Andy should have been one of the most positive days of my year. In fact, it was – until it went sour. I was on the vast anti-war peace march through central London on Saturday, 15 February 2003. I think from the papers there were some 1.5 million of us on the streets, the largest number that has ever marched for any reason at any time in Britain's history. How we could be so comprehensively ignored continues to amaze me.

Mid-morning when I got to the South Bank, Lembit and David were already sharing a bottle of red wine.

'A bit early, isn't it?' I joked, trying to keep things light.

'Get with it, Siân! This is what happens on protest marches,' I was told.

After that, things got better and the atmosphere on the march itself was just incredible. We cheered and chanted and clapped and felt our message had to get across. More prosaically, by the time we got close to the House of Commons I was desperate to go to the loo.

'Can I sneak into your office to use the loo there?' I asked Lembit.

But he said no, because this would have involved him signing me through security and, frankly, he didn't want to go through the rigmarole. In the end, I had to ask one of his researchers to help get me into Portcullis House, where I found a loo.

The plan had been for me to rejoin Lembit and his pals at the Red Lion pub on Whitehall, but he wasn't there. It turned out that, having said he couldn't leave the march, he had in fact followed me into Portcullis House and gone to his office... to raid his drinks cabinet. He must have been at the security desk less than a minute after I was. I was quite upset.

I hung around the pub with Lembit's lovely research assistant, who obviously felt embarrassed. Lembit finally reappeared. He didn't see anything wrong with his behaviour and was pleased that he'd been able to provide booze for his buddy. We found the others and all got on our way again. The march ended in Hyde Park, where we hooked up with Andy Kershaw and listened to some incredible and passionate speeches – Harold Pinter's gave me goose pimples.

As I sat in Hyde Park, I felt that this was conviction politics at its most raw. It was people power; it was about fiery debate, about arguments and history and passion. This was what I had been brought up to be part of, what my parents and my grandparents had always believed in. But somehow for me the reality was so different. My political companion wasn't on the same wavelength that day. He didn't seem to be getting this.

When the speeches wound up, we walked back across Hyde Park and I reminded Lembit of the final part of his day. He was due somewhere in the Home Counties to make a speech to a group of local Lib Dems. I was driving and as usual I was determined not to be late.

'We're going for one drink – we've got time,' he said as Andy led us towards a pub.

Some people never have just one drink. Yet again, I was the good girl, sitting with an orange juice as the others ordered a second round.

'One more, Lembit, then we really have to go,' I said.

'Yeah, yeah.'

But then yet another round.

'Lembit, there's no way we're going to make it. You're the main speaker – you *have* to be there,' I pleaded.

Then Andy said it. 'Look, if the man wants a drink, let him have a drink,' I was told.

It was an incredibly clever comment. Suddenly I was branded the nagging wife, the humourless harridan, a square... It was like some sort of Andy Capp cartoon, with me painted as Flo, the iron-faced killjoy.

Looking back, what amazes me is how hard I worked to ensure Lembit did get to his speeches and fulfil his party responsibilities. I'm not even a party supporter, I'd think. Why am I working harder for them than everyone else? Why am I being an unpaid secretary and chauffeur?

But still Lembit sucked me in. When I managed to get him to his meetings, as I did that night in the Home Counties, he continued to sparkle. Suddenly I would see the passion that had attracted me at the beginning. I could be lifted right back up by his commitment to the party.

Lembit had a Clinton-style ability to work a room. He learns a brief quickly – that's something we always had in common – and he can slice and dice the same old speeches and jokes to fit local issues or personalities. I would sit amazed as his speeches mentioned the names of people he had met, in a crowd, just moments before – I still loved that.

I was still passionate about politics as well. I would quiz Lembit relentlessly about the debates he had sat through and the rumours about the latest Cash for Questions scandals hitting the government. It took me too long to realise he wasn't interested in discussing anything with me. This was a man who wanted to keep it frothy and light, and attend showbiz gigs with me. Maybe he was being discreet, but I got the feeling that often, as with Charles Kennedy's admission of his alcoholism and Mark Oaten's sex scandal, it was me, having got the inside story from our newsroom at ITN, who would keep him up to date. But then it would be Lembit making bad judgements about who to support as the scandals broke. Dating him had not yet given me the political insight I had hoped for. But I still had faith in the man; I still campaigned on his behalf.

In the process, I was always amazed at how little sleep he needed to function and how quickly he could bounce back from one of his heavy drinking nights. In our entire relationship, he never complained once about a hangover.

So why did he drink so much and why did I put up with it?

In some ways, the two questions get the same answer. He drank because he saw no reason not to – he simply didn't have the same restraints of others. Lembit was a man of excesses. I put up with it because for too long I thought I could help him shift gear into adulthood and become a responsible human being, that as an MP he was a role model of sorts. But he was the ultimate in unconventionality. Something in me still responded to that, but this was happening less often.

There is a huge core of amiable anarchy in Lembit. My friend DG always called him a 'genial idiot'. As a politician and as a man, Lembit doesn't believe in checks and balances. He thinks everyone is utterly equal and nothing should be off limits. So, if a middle-aged man wants to hang out at a local club full of teenagers and twenty-something kids, then Lembit feels he should be able to do so without any question, especially if that man is him.

I was always trying to tell him that actions have consequences. I had to remind him that as an MP in modern Britain he did have to consider how things might look. All my years in newsrooms had taught me how little it took to destroy someone's career. I would worry endlessly about how this all this might play in the constituency and beyond. Most of all, I hated it when he wanted to visit some of those nightclubs.

'Can you see Lord Carlile going there?' I once asked, as Lembit waxed lyrical about one local establishment.

But Lembit saw no reason why Alex Carlile, his much-admired predecessor in the constituency, or anyone else might not enjoy the delights of that particular bar. Nor did he see why voters might disapprove of his actions. He always suggested I was too critical, too sensitive and too conventional. The sad truth was that I feared that even the teenagers out on the town of a Friday and Saturday night might be laughing at him. He might become known as the oldest swinger in town. Somehow I persuaded myself to dismiss such thoughts, confident even Lembit wouldn't risk his career to that extent. How wrong I was.

What kept our relationship afloat was the fact that my professional life was on a roll. I had been doing the ITN weather for nearly 15 years but still I was loving it. The words 'climate change' were heard ever more often. And I was on the front line, taking part in documentaries for ITV, the BBC, Channel 4 and even CNN. Doing the same job for so long would get boring if it always stayed the same, but mine was changing all the time.

Having a high profile on the weather gave me plenty of other opportunities to have fun. It let me throw my cares aside sometimes and have a real laugh. Going on a celebrity edition of ITV's *Stars in Their Eyes* in 2003 was a classic example. When I was asked, I thought it had to be a joke. I'm Welsh, so I love to sing, but I'm really far better off in a very big choir, where my shortcomings can be drowned out. I only shine when I'm belting something out at the rugby and my enthusiasm hides the fact that I'm as tone deaf as ever – I'd always remember Stifyn's apt 'pet shop on fire' description.

But they did seem to want me on the show. So I had a challenge: I needed to find a singer who didn't really sing. I found one – Deborah Strickland of the Flying Lizards, who had pretty much spoken her way through the brilliant 'Money (That's What I Want)' in 1979. The other benefit was that very few people knew what Deborah Strickland looked like. All I had in my mind was a vague sense that she looked Germanic and a bit fierce.

Anyway, the whole experience was surreal and hilarious. Shortly afterwards I was asked to go on ITV's *Abbamania* shows, but it seemed the producers had wised up to my voice: they only wanted me as one of the talking heads. Shame! I had always fancied myself as Agnetha.

Don't ask why, but by this point I had also joined the list of unlikely gay icons. Most years Stifyn asked me to join him at Mardi Gras in Cardiff and it was always an incredible party. The best year was when we went on the main stage together and I used Stifyn as a human weather map. I stuck clouds and flashes of lightning on places where the sun rarely shines. We had enough laughs to last for months.

In London, my friends were the bedrock of my life. I was keen to support Ffion Hague and Lisa Graham with Cylch – a circle of friends who would get together for social events and to support Welsh culture. Every few months we would meet en masse and have a great night out. We ate at the chef Bryn Williams's new Odette's restaurant in Primrose Hill; we went to Bryn Terfel's performance of *The Flying Dutchman* at English National Opera and Neil Morrissey's members club Hurst House. Less famous people also got our support. If someone Welsh curated an exhibition at a museum, our Cylch would plan a trip. We enjoyed a fascinating tour of the Egyptology department of the British Museum. If there was an art fair in London, we would congregate at the Welsh stall. It was socialising with a purpose and I heartily recommend it.

Once or twice Lembit joined me in the early days of Cylch. It was nice when he was there, especially when he was in a good mood and ready to join in the fun. But I didn't pine for him when he couldn't make it. Like most busy professional couples, we had to accept that our lives couldn't entirely overlap. The last thing I wanted was to be joined at the hip with my boyfriend. I needed space and Lembit provided that in bucket loads! But he continued to win me over with his grand gestures.

p: Meeting the Queen at the 50th birthday celebration for ITV. I was delighted
 hold her attention for a few minutes. Maybe Lembit thought she shouldn't have
 en chatting about the weather when there were bigger stars to meet…   © *REX Features*

ave been involved with The Prince's Trust for years, and met HRH on
merous occasions, including this presentation with Diane Louise Jordan and
n Sopel (*bottom left*). The Prince and I are both fans of the National Botanic
ardens of Wales (*centre left*).   © *Mirrorpix*

ntre right: The BBC used this photo on their website under the headline
rince views *Final Fantasy* premiere', which was a fund raiser for the Prince's Trust
ymru. But that wasn't all he got to see that night (*bottom right*)! I had no idea
 y dress was so see-through.   © *REX Features / PA Photos*

Raising money for charity has taken me to some truly amazing places.

Top left: On one of the highest peaks of the Himalayas for a Breakthrough Breast Cancer charity walk.

Top right: With Novello on the Great Wall of China.

Centre left: Taking a breather from the trek with pal Timmy.

Centre right: Walking is one of my favourite ways to relax, but the Great Wall of China was a tough challenge, too.

Right: What a reward: coffee in Tiananmen Square after two weeks without. Bliss!

Top: NCH the children's charity does fantastic work for kids all around the UK. I've dressed up in some crazy costumes over the years, and even run through a freezing river for them.

© *NCH the children's charity*

Centre left: I'm always happy to help a good or quirky cause, and opening the attempt to break the world record for the longest phone call landed me in the record books.

© *REX Features*

Centre right: A shot by the Welsh photographer Rhian Ap Gruffydd in a fabulous little black Dolce and Gabbana dress used in a charity calendar.

© *Rhian Ap Gruffydd / Fflic*

Bottom left: With Colin Jackson at the opening ceremony of the Liberty Stadium in Swansea.

© *REX Features*

Clockwise from top left: 2007 was one of my busiest years. Not only did I win a TRIC award for best weather presenter for the second time, but I was named Rear of the Year – with the gorgeous Lee Mead – and continued my work for the Coram Foundation (pictured here at a 2005 Downing St reception with Cherie Blair and my great friend David Goldstone). In the winter I travelled to Kenya for the East African Safari Classic.

© *Capital Pictur*

p left: The first shot of me and Jonathan as a couple made the front page in April 2007.
© *Solo*

p right: Soon, we were being snapped everywhere, including the Canadian Grand Prix.
© *Sutton Images*

ottom: It was a busy summer, with weddings to attend and friends to introduce.
© *Hy Money*

One of mine and Jonathan's first trips abroad was to Nova Scotia in Canada. The fresh air reminded me of home, and the food was something else!

o: Two of my greatest loves! The spectacular Welsh countryside has been an inspiration well as a consolation for me. Cader Idris in Snowdonia has to be one of the most autiful mountains in the world. I am so thrilled to be able to share it with Jonathan.

ttom left: In return, I have accompanied him as his work takes him around the world. this instance in Monaco at the FIA 2007 Gala Prize Giving.

ttom right: Together at the Tamarind restaurant in Mombasa shortly after we engaged.

Happiness at last!

Top left: Feeling more relaxed and more loved than I have in many years.

Top right: Just married: toasting a wonderful day with Bryn Terfel. © *Mike La*

Bottom: Portmeirion in Wales was the perfect place to celebrate our wedding and see out a life-changing year. © *Mike La*

STORM CLOUDS

I joined DG and friends for a wonderful week in Loyd Grossman's house in Kennebunkport, USA – DG had bought the place for a week at a charity auction. Even though he was hundreds of miles away, Lembit managed to spoil things for me. On the Saturday night, we were dining at George Bush's favourite restaurant in the town and having a lovely time. The food was excellent and the pianist played 'Green, Green Grass of Home' in our honour. Then Lembit started ringing me. Clearly, he had been drinking – and drinking for quite I while I thought. Foolishly, I kept taking his calls. He was edgy and I was embarrassed in front of my friends. They could see what was going on but, as usual, I defended him by making some silly excuse and finally switched my phone off. I hid my upset, but he'd succeeded in ruining my night.

On my final day in the States, Lembit called several times to check what flight I was going to be on and when I would be back in Britain. He rang several more times as I made my way back from Heathrow in the slow evening traffic. When I got to the flat, I found out why. I opened the front door and he was standing there, surrounded by hundreds – literally hundreds – of tiny tea-light candles. It was magical and wonderful.

'Hello, Siân, welcome home,' he said, and took me into his arms.

On the nights we were due to be apart he could also pull off a romantic coûp de théatre to keep me in thrall. Some evenings he would fly over from mid-Wales just to have dinner with me for a few hours. Once he joined me for a cup of coffee! He was very good at the big gestures and of course he loved flying. He sprung endless surprises and was still genuinely life enhancing.

Having our house in Wales was also the perfect refuge for us both. We could recharge our batteries there. When the doors were closed, we went back to our old ways. I cooked lots of meals, we played chess; we watched films in front of our log fire... It was companionable and lovely but not entirely without surprises.

One warm night in the summer of 2003 Lembit had a drink or two too many. As we cuddled up on the sofa, he told me how much he loved me, how different I was from anyone he had ever been with before, how much he wanted us to be together for the rest of our lives. But he had a few flashes of self-awareness. He admitted that he stayed out too late sometimes and behaved inconsiderately; he even agreed to a Peter Pan complex. But he said he would change and that he was terrified at the prospect of losing me. From now on in, I was going to see a different Lembit.

Then he moved the conversation on. He started talking about his position in the party and the world. It turned out he really did believe he could get to the top; he always saw himself as a master of the universe when he had been drinking. He talked about being party president and party leader; he talked about government. I humoured him, the way you do to someone when faced with an awkward situation. Then things got even more surreal.

'Carry on my good work if anything ever happens to me,' he told me, suddenly high with drama. 'Will you do that when I'm gone?' He actually started to cry as I tried to work out what he meant.

'You're talking rubbish, Lembit,' I told him.

'No, I'm not. But I have special work to do. You have to

carry it on for me if anything ever happens to me. Siân, promise me that you will.'

Laughably enough, I probably did make some kind of promise, though I never quite got to the bottom of what that special work might be. I thought Lembit was being an idiot as usual. Perhaps he thought he was Gandhi! Certainly, he often compared himself to President Kennedy when it came to excusing his human flaws. Life with him was nothing if not interesting.

Chapter Twelve

Into the Jungle

It was a bit like being asked to become a spy. The call came through early one morning and I was sworn to absolute secrecy. It was early 2003 and I was being sounded out for a place on the next series of *I'm A Celebrity Get Me Out Of Here!* If it was an SAS mission, it couldn't have been treated with more seriousness.

Every year the producers come up with a dream list of people they think will work well together – though in their world 'working well' may well mean rubbing each other up the wrong way or even driving each other mad. Ultimately the show is cast like a prime-time drama and it's all very cloak and dagger. Fortunately, I was doing the weather from the London Television Centre on the South Bank of the Thames, where *I'm A Celebrity*'s producers worked, so we could have as many sneaky meetings as necessary without anyone being any the wiser. I had never really watched the previous series, though like everyone else I was well aware of what a huge show it had been, so I was somewhat bemused to be considered interesting enough for the programme.

I was equally well aware that an appearance could be a risk. People sometimes make fun of weather presenters but we are firmly in the information business and I feel that we do need to be taken seriously. I didn't want to make a total fool of myself in the jungle. But in the end I agreed to go on the show for perhaps the most selfish and superficial of reasons: I was desperate to go to Australia and I couldn't believe that at 43 years old I'd still never been there.

The contract stated that part of the gig involved being given two first-class tickets to Australia. Lembit was over the moon and said he would move heaven and earth to come along. This would be our first proper holiday together and we were going to do it in style. So how could I possibly say no?

Before the final selection takes place, all the possible competitors are sent for psychological tests to the show's psychologist's house, just off Haverstock Hill in North London. The analysts want to check you won't fall apart – or maybe they want to know if you will. They ask how you handle rejection, how you feel about being in a team and being alone, how many friends you have, how close you are to your partner, what sports you played in school, what ambitions you have. Who knows the wrong or right answers to these sorts of questions? But I got through the test with flying colours and met the rest of the celebrities at the London photo-shoot that launched the new line-up.

From the start, I bonded with Phil Tufnell ('Tuffers') because I'm a good Glamorgan girl and I love my cricket.

Danniella Westbrook was someone I would probably never have met in any other circumstances. She's some 15 years younger and, as everyone would find out, she had a lot of demons to fight. But we, too, bonded from the start and I found her fascinating company. She's upfront and honest, and has the utmost integrity. Toyah Willcox and I are pretty much the same age and had plenty in common and Wayne Sleep was as outrageously sharp and funny as I had expected. Cat Deeley was a lovely warm person; John Fashanu ('Fash') was always laughing and, if you are being put in a jungle for two weeks, could you ask for anyone better than a chef like Antony Worrall Thompson ('Wozza')?

The rest of the gang were equally interesting and possibly to the producers' annoyance we all got on. There were no major prima donnas or villains among us. No battles, no huge fights. We supported each other and, apart from a few battles over cigarettes and such like, we all did as we were told. I never watched a single tape of the show but I'm told I hardly featured at all, which I guess was more or less my game plan. I wanted to retain my dignity and draw as little attention to myself as possible.

Everyone flies out at different times depending on their work commitments. The only bad news was that because of the Sars epidemic in Southeast Asia we couldn't have a stopover in Hong Kong. I'd been hoping to take a few Armani suits – my staple on the weather – out with me to have them copied by the tailors out there.

I had Fash, Tuffers and Tara Palmer-Tomkinson – who was there to present the ITV2 programmes – on my flight. I've always been a light packer and all I had with me was a single hand-luggage only case that I put in the overhead locker. Fash found that hilarious – he practically had a trunk. Impressively, TPT had a full set of Louis Vuitton luggage. I was particularly taken by a special tailor-made shoes case. A lady after my own heart!

First class on Singapore Airlines was as good as I hoped, with caviar on tap and fresh orchids everywhere. And the VIP treatment didn't end when we landed. Each of us had our own chauffeurs to drive us from Brisbane airport to the OTT six-star Versace Hotel on the Gold Coast; it truly has to be seen. There seemed to be about a mile of marble and glitz in my vast suite alone. I'm guessing the producers' plan was to wrap us up in such extreme luxury that we suffered even more when we got to the jungle. If so, the Palazzo Versace was certainly the place to be. Not that we had much time to soak it up and laze by the pools.

We did an endless set of photo-shoots and interviews, then had a day out on an island learning how to scale fish and work out which snakes and spiders are poisonous. I paid attention but never did I feel for one moment that ITV would let any really bad ones come near us.

Then it was off to the jungle at last. As a hiker, the three-hour walk to the camp was one of my favourite bits. We could ask our guide questions about the flora and fauna. For all we knew, we might have been walking round and round in circles to try to pad things out and add to the drama. Mind you, we had it easy. In the last series they had to bungee jump into camp – I would definitely have wimped out at that point!

Once more, I proved myself to be the good girl when we were frisked outside the camp. It had never occurred to me to try to break the rules and smuggle anything in. The others had all hidden food and mascara and who knows what else about their persons. I only wish I'd stashed away some thermal underwear. It was one of the coldest and wettest seasons the Gold Coast had had in years. I, of all people, should have been ready for that.

When we got inside, we bagged our beds and tried to come to terms with the fact that this was going to be our home for at least the next seven days and nights. It was like the start of some weirdly competitive cocktail party. Everyone is on a high, trying to get to know each other, to suss each other out and to stake out their own piece of social territory. I think the producers hope we will fall back on our stereotypes, one of us will play the victim, another the loner. One will be the bitch with the heart of gold, another the hard man with the volatile temper and so on. But I couldn't work out what sort of role they had seen fit to allocate to me. I didn't see myself as extreme enough to fit into any particularly exciting box. It didn't worry me: I would just be myself.

Going to the loo with Tuffers in the middle of the night, both of us scared of being in the pitch black, was one big memory of the next few days. In fact, everything to do with the loo seemed to dominate our thoughts in the first week. However good Wozza's food might be, we were all bunged up – and we talked about it at length. 'I've changed my shoes' became code for a job well done. But it took a long time for many of the shoe changes to happen, mine being the longest of all!

I think Fash was one of the first to get a bush-tucker challenge – and from then on he got more and more. Did that mean the public liked or hated him? I couldn't remember. My worst moment was when we found out that the next trial was to be the Bridge of Doom. I was irrationally afraid of even the rope-bridge over to Ant and Dec and the outside world; certainly I didn't want to do any other high-wire act. But I didn't have to. Fash got picked for that one as well. On other days our resident model Catalina was given a crocodile challenge; Wayne's was with rats and Dannie got something with eels. Day after day, somehow I managed to escape. Again, I have no idea if that was because people loved me, hated me or hadn't even noticed me. Whatever, I got away with it.

And I was getting more and more bored. Yes, we had a few tears in the camp and one or two hissy fits. I genuinely felt for Danniella and tried to say what I could to make her feel better about being away from her kids. But apart from that you really do just sit around doing nothing. I'd been told we couldn't have watches, pens or paper in with us. There's nothing to read, nothing to listen to or look at... so I went stir crazy. Every day might produce one captivating hour of prime-time entertainment; the other 23 went very slowly.

People always ask if I learned anything about myself in the camp. I think the environment is so contrived you're unlikely to have some true epiphany. You really can't forget you're on a game show, after all. But if I learned anything it's that I have to be busy. The boredom was the worst bit, that and the fact that you and everything around you reeks of smoke. Keeping that damned fire alight really does become an obsession. Beforehand, the producers make you feel as if the world will end if it goes out. We had plenty more smoke in the camp as well – our smokers seemed to talk about cigarettes 24/7.

Anyway, that first week felt like it lasted a month. I think I was up for eviction with Chris and a couple of others, and when my name was called out I was genuinely pleased to leave. I didn't have some sort of singing career to resurrect in front of the cameras and I wasn't hoping to use the show as a stepping stone to any new television job. It had been a great gig – I'd got my first-class plane tickets and now I could get back to the Versace Hotel and start exploring the Gold Coast and beyond. I certainly didn't feel bad about being the first to leave. Ten days had been quite enough, though even today people think I was there for much longer.

'Siân, you were amazing in that coffin all covered in rats,' I get told.

'Siân, I can't believe you ate those eyeballs,' others say.

'Well done on winning,' someone else told me once.

I remember checking my face in a shop window as I walked away. I like Phil Tufnell, but surely I don't look like him?

For me, the worst part of the week was that final walk over the rope-bridge to meet Ant and Dec. I'm not particularly scared of heights, but I was very glad to get to the end. Ant and Dec were wonderful and I laughed myself silly during and after our interview. They said it had been a very close call between three names and that the votes had gone back and forth furiously. The few clips I saw of my best bits during that eviction programme live on ITV 1 are all I have seen to this day of yours truly on the show! Following this, I was rushed off to talk some more on ITV 2 with Tara Palmer-Tomkinson and Mark Durdon Smith and then propelled into the biggest media circus of my life.

I was the first person to come out and everyone, it seemed, wanted to talk to me. That day I did some 60 interviews. I can't imagine what Phil must have faced when he won. But then I guess being first or last is remembered and possibly better than being an also-ran.

Back in the 'real' world, I got the chance to see the sheer scale of the production. It is jawdropping, a vast, extraordinary city of temporary offices and studios. It really is like *The Truman Show* or a MASH Unit. After speaking to what felt like a million people, I was finally ready to be taken back to the Versace Hotel. And all the time I had just two things on my mind: I want a bath and some decent food that doesn't stink of smoke.

My jeans nearly fell down when I did a live link to *This Morning* with Phil and Fern! I'd lost a huge amount of weight in such a short time. I remember telling them you could get two people in them! And that the first thing I'd eaten when I got back to the opulent luxury of the Versace Hotel was a bacon sandwich.

It was the best I'd ever tasted. And the vast bath I had there the best I ever slipped into. Lembit, bless him, was beaming with excitement when I got back to the hotel. The Welsh Assembly Elections had been on the previous week so he hadn't been able to leave the constituency until then. He touched down just after my eviction was announced. If I had stayed in the jungle, he would have been kicking his heels on his own for up to two weeks. I couldn't believe how much I had genuinely missed him and how good it was to see that lopsided smile. I know he was as thrilled as I was that my early exit meant we could have fun together from the off, and he joined me in as many of the interviews as he could.

The next two weeks were magical. We were given an open-top Audi TT so we could cruise around the coast and we had a driver who took us to Brisbane to an incredible restaurant recommended by Antony Worrall Thompson. Tim Vincent was on standby to go on the show in case someone dropped out. Lucky so and so, he had been hanging around Sydney having a ball while the rest of us were in the camp.

And as other people got voted off the show we had even more fun. Lembit and I went to dinner with Toyah and her husband Robert Fripp; we met up with Danniella and her husband Kevin, plus all the others. I think the whole experience was so bizarre that you have to be a bit hysterical about it. We would probably have made far better viewing after the show than we did when we were on it.

Lembit and I were also on a roll. We holidayed well together and I was head over heels in love with Australia – all my expectations about the country had been met. Later, we met up with the gang again for the reunion show. We laughed so much on that first holiday we had together. We shared some incredible times and built some wonderful memories. How lucky can you be?

Chapter Thriteen
Fixing Things

The fixer in me had certainly taken on quite a challenge in Lembit. But I've never been a quitter, so I reckoned I always stood a chance of winning the battle. My key task was to change the way he and I organised our time. For well over a year, we had been living together but because we were both so busy we could go several days without seeing each other.

That wouldn't matter if it was planned in advance but Lembit was so disorganised I never knew what he would be doing from one day to the next. I remember saying goodbye to him in London one morning as I headed off to ITN. Later that day I rang him on his mobile and asked if he was coming back in time for dinner.

'I can't – I'm in Toulouse for a meeting,' he told me.

I laughed out loud, but it was ridiculous that he had left the country without telling me. I knew we had to sort this out.

'Can't we just compare diaries every week, or whenever we're together?' I asked when he was back in the flat.

'But my diary is too fluid. It changes all the time.'

'Well, some things in it have to be fixed – the speeches you are giving and the meetings you need to attend. I need to know about them if you want me to drive you there.'

'But we've managed fine so far.'

'Yes, but only because I've cancelled things to make sure we manage,' I said. 'We only manage because of my good will.'

But I know Lembit didn't really take it in. Perhaps he stopped listening at the start of the conversation. I thought I could open up a new front in the battle. If Lembit wouldn't help, then I could always tackle his Parliamentary and Constituency offices: one would assume that they must know where he was going to be on any given day. But, in view of how little I knew, I speculated on whether his staff would be told the full story of his whereabouts. Once more, I was knocked back: they admitted that half the time they weren't even in the loop themselves.

'How do you and William organise your diaries?' I asked Ffion Hague during a girlie lunch at the members' club Home House in London. I have known her for years and I remember how puzzled she looked at the question. It turned out she and William simply talked about things. They always knew where they would both be and when; they shared things – that was what normal people did and that's what I had always done in the past.

But I brushed it under the carpet. I still loved Lembit's wildness and his unpredictability. I told myself there was nothing sinister about the big gaps in his diary. After all, it wasn't as if he was cheating on me. Was it?

I got a partial answer to that question in December of that year – and it wasn't the one I wanted.

Two of my closest friends, Novello and Ron Noades, were having a dinner party at their house in Purley in Surrey. Ingrid Tarrant, James Baker, Russell Miller and Tim Thorne would be there as well. Despite ongoing arguments over his diary, Lembit promised to keep the date free so we could both get to the party. And I know he wanted to be there – Novello and Ron are wonderful hosts and we've had plenty of great evenings with them over the years. They had welcomed Lembit into our gang from the start and I knew he was comfortable with them. But events looked set to get in the way...

A week before the party Lembit got back to my flat with a grim look on his face. Around Christmas almost 100 redundancies were announced at a factory in his constituency. Talks were arranged for the day after the party. Lembit had been asked to attend and he could hardly refuse. Jobs were at stake and this was what being an MP ought to be all about. Of course, his priority had to be his constituents.

I said I would go to Novello and Ron's on my own but Lembit reckoned he could still make it.

'If you drive us down to the party we can get up at five the next morning and I'll drive us back up to mid-Wales so I can get to the meeting,' he suggested.

It seemed like a mad plan and I can't say I liked the idea of a 5am alarm call, but I agreed as I always did.

The dinner and the company were perfect, just at I had

known they would be. I love sitting around a table with old friends. Talking and eating are my two favourite pastimes.

From the start, I had known that he was tense but I put it down to worries about the next day's meetings – it was that period between Christmas and the New Year, after all. Anything he could do to cut the number of redundancies would make a huge difference in his constituency. But worries about work don't excuse rudeness and by 10pm he crossed a line. Lembit was no longer just joking along with people and sharing in the fun, he had started to interrupt other people's conversations and play the fool. That was the first time Ingrid had met my new man and I so wanted her to like him. Much later, she told me that she thought he was a complete idiot.

Lembit never really liked it when the spotlight descended on other people. When he was on top form, he was so charming that he was guaranteed to get all the attention. And when he wasn't he could sometimes behave in a way that spoiled everything for the rest of us. This was clearly one of those nights so I decided to cut my losses while I was ahead.

I reminded everyone about our ridiculously early start then said my goodnights and headed to our room. I assumed Lembit would take the hint and follow – but he didn't. Upstairs I set my mobile to go off for our 5am departure and resigned myself to doing the driving. I was worried that, despite his promises, Lembit might still have too much booze in his system to drive the next morning.

But where was he?

After about an hour I was dozing slightly, but woke up to hear Lembit telling someone in no uncertain terms how the planet could be destroyed and we would have no way to defend ourselves. What a long time it seemed since I had found those asteroid stories so endearing. And how loud he must be shouting for me to hear him up in our room. I was mortified on his behalf. What an old bore he had turned into all of sudden!

An hour later, I woke up again. More loud discussions were going on downstairs, with Lembit still very much in the chair. I was furious. We had a deal about how the next day was going to work out: Lembit had already broken it by drinking too much. I turned off the alarm on my phone. Sod it, I thought. If he wants to be irresponsible, then he has to face the consequences on his own! I can't mother him forever.

But the night from hell wasn't over yet. The next time I woke it was to hear a crash from our en suite bathroom. Then I heard it again. Lembit was in the bathroom crashing about and I heard a sound like someone dropping a mobile phone on the tiled floor. It was 2am. Against my better judgement, I decided to leave him to it and go back to sleep. The next thing that woke me was not a noise, but silence. It was gone 3am and the bathroom was quiet. Had something happened to him? I was desperately tired and furious with him for ruining the night, but I still climbed out of bed to check. I stood and looked at him in the harsh bathroom light. He looked like a sad, grey old man. He had passed out, sitting on the toilet, with his head slumped forward and a ridiculous smile on his face. His phone was on the floor, having fallen from his hand one last time. If he had backache in the morning, it would serve him right. But I did pick up his phone. Who had been texting at 3am?

And was I justified in looking through his sent folder to find out? Of course I damn well was! I clicked on to it straightaway. Though his sent folder was empty, his inbox was full.

Some messages were affectionate and intimate in tone. One mentioned the words Puppy dog; another what I took to be requests to meet up at a later date. It could have been some random mobile phone spam, but the fact that his sent folder was entirely empty lead me to believe otherwise. They certainly didn't sound like his mum.

'Lembit, get up!' I tried to drag him out of the en suite and into the bedroom.

Breakfast the next morning was a spectacularly tense affair. Lembit and I were unexpected guests, having told our hosts we would have left by dawn. But Ron and Novello and Tim tried to act as if everything was normal. Novello makes the best coffee of anyone I know, but it wasn't enough to help the conversation flow. Lembit was sitting there looking like death in last night's crumpled clothes. Everyone was aware of the atmosphere but no one felt they could say anything.

Even Lembit had accepted at this point that I was unlikely to spend the next four hours driving him to Wales. And by then he had clearly missed his important meeting. I had driven down to Purley in the pouring rain the previous evening and kept my end of the bargain. If he wanted to get there, he would have to find a train. All I was prepared to do was to take him to the station. I gave Tim a lift as well, and the atmosphere in the car was no better than it had been around the breakfast table.

Tim said his goodbyes as Lembit climbed out of the car and slammed the door behind him. He didn't kiss me

goodbye or say a word as he headed off to the platform.
I have never been so pleased to see the back of anyone in
my life. And I made a mental note to ring Tim later on –
I should apologise for leaving him with Lembit. I didn't
expect he would be a great travelling companion that day.

I got the car in gear and drove round the corner where I
couldn't be seen. From there, I called my old friend
Veronica in Newtown. I needed advice, so I told her
everything. She is a fair, kind woman, but she could hardly
have been clearer in her response.

'Look, Siân, if he's making you so unhappy and you
don't think it's going to get better you can just leave him.
Get him to pack his bags and move out of your flat.'

They were uncompromising words. I got more of the
same over the next few days when I called Eileen in
Cornwall, Trish Bertram, Stifyn and my other close
friends. But for some reason I still wasn't ready to hear it.

I think I was in denial about the thought that Lembit
might be on the skids. Honesty, trust and respect had
always been central to my previous relationships and I had
taken it as a given in this one as well. I simply couldn't
believe I had been wrong, so I didn't let myself believe it. I
carried on regardless. I trusted the fact that he was well
and truly ashamed of himself.

I drove back to London and did my next set of ITN
weather shifts as if nothing had happened. It was up to
Lembit to make the first move. He owed me a very big
apology and I was determined to get one. Soon I did. It
arrived by text and amounted to little more than a few
hastily typed words, but I suppose beggars can't be
choosers. Then I got a flurry of the old 'I love you' texts.

Against my better judgement, they made me smile. I was kicking myself, but, however badly he had behaved, something was still there. Things had been so much fun at the start that a huge part of me didn't want our roller-coaster ride of a relationship to end.

It seemed Lembit agreed. From this point on, he started leaving a series of increasingly frantic voice messages saying we would spend more time together in the future. He said we could go back to the good days when we had gone to the cinema and grabbed takeaways and had fun – like proper couples; he made some lovely promises, all of which I ignored. I vowed not to speak to him again.

But then I weakened. Don't we women always weaken? One day I picked up the phone when I saw his number. I listened to his latest, greatest declarations of love. I softened up and then he played his ace: he's a clever man and he appealed to the fixer in me.

'I can change, you know I can. You've already helped me so much. Please don't give up on us now. I need your help if I'm to make it,' he begged. Then he turned on the charm and buttered me up in flattery. He went on and on about how he admired my strength, my resolution, my character... Of course, it was all nonsense but he wrapped me up and reeled me in with the words.

'I love you, I love you, I love you,' he repeated again and again. Just like he always did when the road got rough. So I caved in and gave Lembit another chance. I believed him when he said he would change. Two months later when he proposed to me I said 'yes'. What was I thinking? Why on earth was I such a fool?

Chapter Fourteen

The Proposal

We were on the way back from a Lib Dem meeting in Norfolk when Lembit first mentioned marriage, but it was hardly the most romantic of moments. We were in the car (I was driving), it was late and we were both exhausted. That said, I felt we were making real progress as a couple: we were back on an even keel again, content in each other's company. And he did seem to be following through on his promises to change.

Lembit was certainly looking good that evening. I had picked out a dark-blue Paul Smith suit, an M&S pink shirt and an Armani tie. He looked professional, confident and successful; he looked like a contender.

'You've done wonders with him,' an elderly lady in purple told me, as I watched him work his way round the room before the dinner. 'We've all noticed. Since you've been with Lembit, he's blossomed. He just needed a woman's touch.'

I had heard those sorts of sentiments right back at the beginning of our relationship in the constituency and in London. It felt good to hear them again in quite a different environment. That night I had witnessed plenty more flashes of the Lembit that I had fallen for right at the start. As we moved around the room, I listened in on his conversations, hearing a few words of the small talk he made as he approached the top table. A quick question here, a vague enquiry there... I knew the answers would be stored up in his mind. He would then weave all the local issues into his speech.

It was a gift. His standard after-dinner speech was an off-the-peg suit, but these titbits of last-minute information made it a bespoke, tailor-made alternative, as if every word had been written especially for the people in the room that night.

As usual, he didn't touch a drop of wine throughout the dinner, though I broke my 'no caffeine after six' rule and needed two black coffees to see me through the evening. Then he delivered his speech with all the right local mentions. It was stunning, special... He was the consummate politician. As I joined in the applause, I congratulated myself on forgiving him and staying at his side. There is something hypnotic about being in a room with someone that everyone else thinks is a genius and a visionary – you start to believe it yourself. So I forgot about all the bad times and allowed myself to be swept along with the others. Lembit and I were right to put the past behind us, I decided. He could still achieve great things.

When we finally got to talk in a little huddle after the meal, Lembit was desperate for feedback on the speech –

just as he always was. 'What was I like? Did the joke about the toilets go down well? Did everyone laugh? Who was laughing? Did people get the jokes? Was I good?' And so it went on.

I told him that he had been a star and was loved by all. And I meant it. His face broke out into the most enormous smile. Suddenly, he held my hand. 'I was good, wasn't I?' he asked again.

'Yes, you were.'

And then he said it. 'I know it's getting late. There's one more set of people I really have to speak to, but after that we'll go.'

I watched him do his final piece of glad-handing. If we did indeed leave this would be a first: it would be a breakthrough for us as a couple. In the past he always stayed until the bitter end, sometimes drinking copiously, no matter how early either of us had to get up for work the following morning. Often we would be quite literally the last to leave, practically turning the lights off in our wake. Whenever he promised to leave in good time, normally because I was on an early the next day, he would always break his promise and stay anyway.

But tonight I watched him deliberately cut the evening short. He made sure his hosts knew that when he said goodnight he meant it. And he was doing it for me. We left the hall earlier than we had left any political meeting in our entire relationship, and he wasn't even tipsy. It was such a small thing but it meant a huge amount to me.

Tired but happy, I drove us home. A relationship has to be about sacrifices and compromises and Lembit was finally beginning to appreciate his part of the deal. He was on a high from the speech and I was on a high because he was clearly making an effort. Perhaps what happened next was inevitable.

'We're a good team, aren't we?' he asked suddenly. I actually thought he had nodded off in the passenger seat. 'We work so well together. We should get married...'

At that exact moment, I had just pulled out into the fast lane to overtake another car. It could all have gone horribly wrong, but I slowed down and regrouped.

'Lembit, is that a proposal?'

'Yes, but I'm going to do it so much better later.'

Moments later, he was asleep and I was in a state of shock. I had never actively looked for marriage. My long stable relationships had always been good enough in themselves. My mother always instilled an important sense of self into me. She made me feel I could always be complete on my own, that I didn't need to be married to feel whole.

But Lembit had always been different, so maybe our relationship should follow a different course as well. I've always been excited by the thrill of the new. So, while I had absolutely no idea whether I would say yes or no, I decided to savour this little development. If Lembit really did intend to propose properly one day then I would be ready for him. I just hoped I would know what to say when the moment came.

'We have to spend Valentine's Day together.' It was an unusually romantic instruction from Lembit. 'I won't have any Parliamentary work to do in the evening. Keep your diary clear as well. We can have dinner together, just the two of us. Wouldn't Valentine's Day be a great date to become engaged?'

He left the room, smiling, before I could reply. And I felt a rush of affection for him. The drinking and the disappearances didn't seem to matter any more. This was the old Lembit: the one who swept me off my feet at the beginning with his madness, his enthusiasm and his grandiose romantic gestures. I thought back to the nights in my flat with all the candles and the charmer who serenaded me in the moonlight. The times he had said 'I love you' almost until he was hoarse.

When 14 February came around, I cleaned the flat from top to bottom. I bought some heart-shaped fairy lights and hung them round the mirror in the living room. I also bought heart-shaped cheeses and, at 7.30 when Lembit was due home, I checked my dress and hair, and lit the candles on the dinner table. I still wasn't sure if I wanted to get married; I just wanted everything to be perfect for a nice, romantic meal.

But where was Lembit?

At eight, I called his mobile. No reply. At 8.30 I texted. Again, nothing. At 9.30 I called and texted again. Could he have been in an accident? Had something happened?

In the end I started to laugh. Lembit was absolutely infuriating. He had made a huge deal out of this and then forgotten all about it, just as he always did. It was a good job I was treating the whole engagement thing as a joke, that I wasn't desperate to get a ring on my finger.

So I did what felt right. I rang up my friend Trish and we headed out to the pub for a few drinks on our own. We had a lovely night. Who needs unreliable men? And were any men as unreliable as mine? Lembit hadn't called by the time Trish and I left the pub and he wasn't back at the flat when I got home. So I finished off the tidying up and went to bed.

As I lay in bed I remembered something he had told me at the start of our relationship. 'My family isn't very good at marriage,' he had said, after explaining that all three living generations of Opiks, his grandparents, parents, sister and his brother, had all been divorced. Forget being married, I thought with a wry smile, it seemed Lembit wasn't even any good at proposing!

It was two in the morning when I heard his key being pushed into the lock. Then there was some swearing, some bumping and some more noise before finally the door flew open. It slammed shut. He headed towards the bedroom, bringing a cloud of alcohol and cigarette smoke along with him. 'Where have you been?' I was trying to keep it light. The last thing I wanted was an argument, especially since I had an early start the next day.

'Siân, that's information you don't need to know.'

Was that some kind of joke? What kind of bizarre new catchphrase was this? A few days later, I found out the truth. He and Charles Kennedy had been having a good time at the BBC 2 Folk Awards.

Forget about getting married. We were going on a holiday. Planning a great trip always takes my mind off my troubles. So that's what I did after putting the Valentine's Day debacle behind me. I had started doing some travel writing for the *Mail on Sunday* and had been given the chance to try out a fantastic cruise to St Petersburg.

THE PROPOSAL

Lembit and I liked travelling together – we both loved seeing new places and on the whole everything was more relaxed away from the pressures of the TV studios, the debating chambers and the constituency. So we had good times on both cruises we took on the chic little *Hebridean Spirit*. The food was as good as the views and the staff superb.

When you are out on the ocean the skies tend to be incredibly clear. Lembit and I spent a lot of time stargazing. As we tried to name all the constellations one night, he pulled me close. He's so tall and it felt good to be wrapped up against him.

'This is really romantic. It would be a good place to propose,' he said.

But still he didn't.

Instead, we just carried on looking at the skies and then headed back to our cabin.

The rest of the trip was just as relaxed and calm. I was even prepared to laugh a little about his latest proposal about a proposal. It was a bit like all the talks about talks that had led up to the Northern Ireland peace process. Are all politicians this complicated? I made a mental note to ask Ffion how William had proposed to her. Somehow I had a feeling it would have been done a little more smoothly.

Our next halfway-house proposal came when I was caught up on another wave of nostalgia for the early days of my relationship with Lembit: we were 4,000 feet up in the air in his plane. We had taken off from my favourite little Welshpool airport and gazing out over stunning Welsh mountains. The most beautiful country, it looks totally different from the air.

I turned to look at Lembit and he was smiling broadly. He looked happier than he had been in years. It was the Lembit of old once more, the one I had fallen for at the start.

'Siân, here I am, doing what I love, above an area I love, with the woman I love. The only thing that would make this more perfect is for us to get married,' he said.

Now it was my turn to smile.

It was another proposal about a proposal, another statement that wasn't quite a question. Looking back, I think he was subconsciously trying to protect himself from rejection. If he never quite asked the question, I could never quite turn him down. I think his idea was that if he floated the words around often enough I would simply run with them and say 'yes' anyway. Then we could just get on with it. Who says romance is dead? Anyway, I'm embarrassed to say that this is pretty much how it worked out.

I never did get a firm proposal; I never got a concrete question. Lembit certainly never had the sense of style to go down on one knee. So I never really said 'yes' to him either.

'I went down on one wing,' Lembit told the press on one occasion, and they ran with it. It was a lovely line, but that's all it was. In reality, we just drifted into our engagement. We decided that we would get married without ever properly putting it into words. How weird is that? That night back at the house we had rare Welsh black beefsteak and champagne as a mini-celebration for our mini-non-proposal. The next day I rang my mother from the car on the M4 and then phoned all my friends.

It all felt like a bit of a laugh. Neither Lembit nor I was a conventional person so maybe our non-conventional engagement would work out all right in the end. It wasn't as if we had any intention of tying the knot in the near future. I knew from the start that this could be one of the longest engagements on record, particularly as his suggestions of marriage were all fairly nebulous. Every time he did a dinner and his speech went down well, he'd be so ecstatic that he would clasp me tightly and say we were a great double act and we should marry. He liked the fact that his audience at these dinners liked me and, of course, that I drove him back and forth to these events. He would mention the 'M' word when he was on a high like that. Ditto after a successful gig in his constituency, because locally they always liked seeing me with him. There was a genuine feeling that I was good for him and people loved seeing us together.

'Weather girl sets date to marry MP,' went the headline. It was nice to be noticed. But the story wasn't exactly accurate because we hadn't even begun to think about wedding dates. Lembit hadn't even bought a ring and I didn't really expect him to. Like most of our domestic issues, that too was going to be up to me.

My dream was to have a ring made from Welsh gold, but it's hard to get hold of because they don't mine it any more. So I went online and found three places that dealt in it, one of which was in Machynlleth, in Lembit's constituency and one of my favourite towns in Wales. That had to be a good sign. I owned a large heart-shaped diamond and I agreed that this could go on the new ring. Lembit was always strapped for cash so this would make it easier for him. He paid for the gold, which came to around £700. I think it was a little more than he had been expecting to pay.

But Welsh gold, like Welsh women, comes at a premium. And surely we're worth it!

'*Really*? They want us?' It was late May 2004 and I was on the phone to my agent. Lembit and I been asked to do a shoot in *Hello!* about our engagement. They wanted pictures and a joint interview with the happy couple.

Having never quite seen myself as a typical celebrity, I couldn't quite believe *Hello!* could really be interested in our news. But Lembit was flattered and very keen to do it. When I told him about the request, he positively glowed. He loved seeing his name in print and clearly thought this would do his electoral prospects the power of good.

We were both still on a high after going public on the engagement. The number of cards we had been sent defied belief. Dozens upon dozens arrived every day – from friends, family, fans, constituents and all sorts of other people in Britain and beyond. I felt as if I was riding a wave of goodwill. We ourselves might not have taken the engagement very seriously, but everyone else seemed to be. It was lovely that so many people believed in us as a couple; complete strangers gave me hugs and kisses in the street and said they knew we would be very happy together. We could have opened a florist with all our flowers. It was a bit like being brainwashed.

It didn't take Lembit or me long to decide where we should do the *Hello!* interview. We chose Llangoed Hall in Powys. It is a glorious country-house hotel owned by the family of my very good friend Jane Ashley. I knew a lot of the staff there and had also asked Mark Coray to come up from Cardiff to do his usual magic with my hair. Another old friend, Astrid Kearney, was there to do my make-up. I was childishly excited about the whole thing.

But it all went wrong.

Astrid and I had arrived the night before and Lembit was due to join us for dinner. But Lembit was late, as usual, and in a mood.

Lembit had his old hangdog expression on his face and was barely communicative as he stomped up to the hotel lounge. Astrid and I were sitting in front of a huge log fire, chatting away to our hearts' content. Something had probably gone wrong in the Cardiff meeting he'd come from but I was frustrated that he couldn't snap out of it for me. He was still moody the next day and, as the first sets of photos were taken, we barely spoke. The distance between us was physical, as well as mental.

'Go on, put your arm around her! You are going to be marrying her, after all.'

How humiliating that it required a magazine photographer to say that to my fiancé.

But, while Lembit did then manage to raise some smiles with a dramatic comedy hug, it was hardly the most spontaneous or relaxed of afternoons. We had to change clothes half a dozen times and were pictured in several different rooms and out on the terrace having tea. But the longer the shoot lasted, the more the tension seemed to mount. I look at those pictures today and hardly recognise myself. That brittle red-haired woman looks like a complete stranger. At the time, I felt as if I was being shown up in front of Mark and Astrid. And I couldn't pretend that it had gone unnoticed.

'What's up with Lembit? He didn't touch you all day. He

didn't put his arm around you; he didn't even give you a peck on the cheek. Nothing.' That was Astrid's take when the shoot was over and my sulking fiancé had driven off on his own.

We were heading back to London in my car on the M4. Astrid is an old friend: she's incredibly intuitive and creative and has an innate ability to read people's body language. She had read Lembit's loud and clear.

I had no idea what to say. And I knew there would be no point asking Lembit about it next time we met. If there was any explanation at all, he would probably decide it was 'information that I did not need to know'. That infuriatingly smug phrase was cropping up more and more frequently in our conversations. Why on earth did he think it was a clever thing to say? After dropping Astrid off and heading home, I did a lot of thinking. I was so frustrated that the Lembit who made everyone smile seemed to have temporarily disappeared from view; I couldn't understand why he was always sulking when we were out with friends and colleagues. Something had to change.

I vowed to put him on notice. We weren't planning to get married in a hurry – we were thinking the spring or summer of 2005 at the earliest. In that time, Lembit would just have to turn things around. I wanted him to forget about all his worries and bring back the sparkle and the fun that had dazzled me from the start. He would have to shape up or ship out, as they say.

The big story that kept Lembit's mind off our wedding plans that summer was his long-awaited bid for the Lib Dem Presidency – long-awaited by *him*, I should add. The party, I fear, would be distinctly underwhelmed. The current president, Lord Dholakia, was standing down at the end of his four-year term and Lembit was determined to take over. The Presidency was pretty much just a figurehead role, but I suspected it was the first step in his plan to become party leader.

Against my better judgement, I liked the fact that he was still feeling ambitious. You had to admire his self-belief especially as he was up against party favourite Simon Hughes. In June, we launched the bid to the press at Westminster. I was a tad upset because I'd just discovered his election pamphlet declared he 'might be engaged to Siân, but was married to the party'. Subtle, hey? 'Sunny days are ahead,' I told the press, or some such nonsense. Then the schmoozing and the glad-handing and the campaigning began.

We spent a couple of months flogging this particular dead horse but in September the party members put us out of our misery. Simon Hughes won by a mile.

Far from the public eye, we had lived through another challenge that year. At the ripe old age of 45, I found out that I was pregnant with Lembit's child.

Until then the idea of becoming a mother had never seemed very real to me. In my twenties and thirties, I didn't have the all-consuming urge to have children that I have seen in some friends and colleagues. I was building up a team of nieces and nephews that I loved. I'm a proud godmother to Morgan and Tallulah Thomas, the two children of my old friends Julie and Dyfed, and to Mark Cavendish's niece, Sarah. But I was ambivalent about having children of my own. In the right relationship at the right time, I think they may well have been wonderful, and I certainly wasn't going to have children for the sake of it. I had my usual laissez-faire attitude to parenthood – the same laissez-faire attitude I have always had to my career and my life in general. I would take what comes and in the meantime I would enjoy the moment. I could hardly complain about the way my life had worked out. I had no right to be miserable about anything. When I hit my forties, I pretty much thought I would never be a mother and that was absolutely fine.

So I was stunned, quite staggered in fact, when I found I was pregnant in 2004. I was scared as well. Many of my friends had suffered miscarriages and I knew that I couldn't take anything for granted at that age. In fact, the whole thing seemed quite extraordinary. But as the days passed I warmed to the idea, though I took nothing for granted.

Lembit had taken the news in his own inimitable fashion. 'I knew already,' he told me. 'I had sensed it.' Apparently psychic powers – and healing hands – ran in his family. It must be an old Estonian thing. And to his credit, he was very pleased and excited. 'I knew we were going to have a baby,' he said. And he couldn't stop smiling.

But it wasn't to be. Some six or seven weeks later, I had some scans on Harley Street that indicated I would miscarry.

Lembit was at his constituency in Wales when I was admitted into University College Hospital in central London. There, I spent a grim night in a little room just off the main ward. Lembit called my parents and kept them updated on my news. Then he rushed down to London for a late-night visit.

The following day he was back at the hospital to help me

get home. He was subdued and seemed very tired, but the outer-worldly, mad professor in him meant his definition of 'help' varied slightly from mine. 'We can get a bus from here, can't we?' he asked, as we headed out of the hospital on to Tottenham Court Road.

'No, Lembit, we bloody well can't! We're getting a taxi,' I retorted. And, as usual, I paid for it.

I was lucky to be able to bounce back from the miscarriage. Physically I was fine, and mentally I think my circumstances helped. I hadn't been trying for a child so the loss was easier to bear. Ultimately, I don't think we can all have everything we want in life. If some things don't come to us, then we have to focus on all the other good things that do. And my life was so full of other joys and opportunities. In 2004 it was also packed with new challenges.

I had persuaded my trekking gang to sign up for the big one. We were walking the Great Wall of China – or at least a decent enough stretch of it. And we were a tough, fit bunch – worryingly so, as far as I was concerned. Novello plays golf almost every day and would later go on to do a lung-busting expedition to the North Pole with her mate Ian Wright the following June, so she wasn't going to have any problems keeping up. My old ITN colleague James Baker used to row for Wales, so his legs and lungs were in pretty good nick, and Floella Benjamin runs marathons. The rest of us – Russell Christie, Chris Roberts, Chris Jones, Baden Hall and Tim Thorne – had all been in training too, as had Ingrid Tarrant, though in the end she had to pull out at the last moment when a big work commitment came up.

As soon as we got going, the magic began. We passed

through tiny villages where most of the people had never seen Europeans before. And we were invited into people's homes; we were entertained and offered food and drink by people with next to nothing.

Parts of the Wall are just as you imagine it from schoolbooks, while in other areas there is pretty much nothing left but a path. There were some tough gradients, but our group took them in our stride. We laughed our way up the hills and then we laughed our way back down them. Even on the tougher parts, we managed to joke. At one point, we had to flatten ourselves against a rock face and edge along a tiny ledge. I took my gloves off to get a better grip and placed my hands flat on the rocks.

'Siân, what a gorgeous manicure you have!' joked one of the Tims as we inched across.

'Get a move on. This is not the time for idle chit-chat!' the girls behind screamed, as they queued up behind us on our precarious ledge.

Overall, we covered some 60 miles of high elevation and raised tens of thousands of pounds for NCH. By the end, we all felt incredibly emotional. Although already the best of friends, we really bonded on that trip. Those memories will last forever. And, with the walking done, it was time to relax.

One of my favourite photographs – which I have included in this book – is of a group of us girls clutching Starbucks coffee cups in Tiananmen Square in Beijing. We had been so desperate for a coffee after a fortnight without that we practically pushed people aside to get through the door. A desert oasis couldn't have looked more attractive to a thirsty man than a vente latte seemed to us that day. I heard recently that the Starbucks is being closed down –

too Western for such a historic area, apparently. Most of
me can see the point. But, oh boy, was I glad it was there
after our trek!

In Beijing, I am a little ashamed to admit that we were
all desperate for a burger as well. I try to be the queen of
eating the right food in the right places, I try to support
local food and farmers' markets, but after 10 days on the
road in China even I was desperate for a big old Western
meal. So, on the final night, after seeing the Forbidden City
and going a bit wild on the market stalls selling mock,
knock-off Gucci and Prada kit, we skipped the Peking
Opera for a slap-up dinner in a five-star hotel. Naughty,
but oh so nice!

Chapter Fifteen

Grief

In July 2004, Lembit's father, Uno, had stumbled on the beach in Weston-super-Mare and broken his leg. After that, his strength just wouldn't come back. He discovered he couldn't whistle any more and found keeping his balance difficult. Eventually he was diagnosed with Motor Neurone Disease.

The prognosis was not good: the illness is progressive and Uno was told he was unlikely to have much more than two years to live. I think I took the news almost as badly as Lembit. I had always liked Uno – he was an academic and a kind and honourable man. But Lembit and his father had their differences and I feared he would bury his head in the sand, as he so often did.

'Lembit, you have to visit him.'

His stepmother Ene and I both tried to get the message across, but Lembit had a complicated relationship with his dad. He could still have been angry that Uno had left his mother and remarried, even though he waited until his children were grown before leaving.

As the months passed and Ene told me how quickly Uno was deteriorating, I knew I had to be strong on Lembit's behalf. There was no longer time to pussyfoot about. 'Lembit, your father is dying. If you don't go and see him now you may never see him again,' I told him.

It was a battle and probably the only one I ever won with Lembit. I'm proud to say I did succeed in getting him to visit more often.

Motor Neurone Disease is an awful illness, especially for someone as intelligent as Lembit's dad. It traps your mind inside your body. Your muscles waste away and you become unable to walk, talk or feed yourself. But your brain is active so you know exactly what is happening. For a proud, intelligent man like Uno the effect of Motor Neurone Disease was just unbearably cruel. And I felt so much for his wonderful wife Ene. He had at last found happiness in his life with her and to see two people in their seventies so very much in love was inspiring. She was his rock.

I remember helping with the food at Uno's funeral. I was thinking how important family ties are and how we don't always appreciate the older generation until they are gone. We don't ask them enough questions, then one day we wake up and it's too late.

The funeral promised to be a very important day for Lembit. It had been an exhausting week for him, with the General Election just four days before, and I wanted to do my best to help him deal with it. On the way down to Wiltshire from mid-Wales, he had made me a promise: in honour of his father, he wouldn't drink. I held his hand briefly as he said it. This was absolutely the right thing to do and I was proud of him. His father would really have valued that promise.

To be absolutely honest, I had another reason for wanting him to stay off drink, however. We both had ridiculously early starts at work the next day. I had a 7am call for make-up in London and was desperate to get as much sleep as possible beforehand. We agreed we would leave by 10pm. Why I ever thought this would happen, I don't know.

Events overtook Lembit almost straight away. From the moment his sister Urve sent out for extra supplies of alcohol, my heart sank. It was an extraordinarily testing time for him, it's true. I spotted him knocking something over across the room and everything, suddenly, felt bleak and cold. I prayed he would be sensible, that he would have the strength to stop after one. He had made the pledge in good faith, of course, and hadn't meant to be disloyal, but he had a second and then a third drink and I became incredibly unhappy.

'What are you doing? You said you wouldn't drink!' I whispered at him, at one point. As usual, he ignored me.

Our 10pm deadline came and went. By 11pm, he was playing his harmonica. Every time I could get close to him, I reminded him we had to leave; that it was so late and we needed to go. Then I made my threat: 'I'm going to leave on my own soon. This is getting out of hand...'

Clearly, I had made this kind of threat far too many times in the past and I had never followed through. The Siân Lloyd free taxi service always waited around till the bitter end of all the ugly, drunken evenings. That's probably why there had been so many of them. But that evening my car service shut up shop. I told Lembit one more time that I was going home and I said my goodbyes, with sympathy, to his family. Then I walked away to my car.

For a while, I sat there, ringing his mobile just in case I could persuade him to join me. But he didn't answer. I went back into the hall and still he refused to come. So I headed back to London on my own. I know Urve thought this was harsh on my part, but she didn't know our history. She didn't know how many promises I had been made in the past. Or that all of them had been broken. When I got back to the London flat, there was a message on my answering machine from Lembit. Absurd as it seems now, he claimed he was going to destroy my career and that he would make sure I never worked again. No doubt it could all have been hot air, but at the time it was very upsetting. I deleted it, and immediately felt a lot better, though I wonder what his reaction would have been if I had ever played it to him – he sounded so menacing.

Fool that I am, I let Lembit off the hook yet again when he finally got back from the funeral the next day. But I had to – I couldn't chide a man who had just lost his father. Anyway, the roller-coaster ride of our relationship was still going full pelt. Above everything, I wanted to help him deal with the loss of his father.

We took refuge in the house in mid-Wales and against all odds we started to get along a little better. We went out walking, we watched lots of old movies and I cooked all his favourite dishes – steak with gratin Dauphinoise, beef

Stroganoff, pasta with four cheeses, homemade pizza with masses of anchovies and sausages with onion gravy and mustard mash. Friends noticed we were more stable than we'd been in a long while. I think I was able to provide some comfort for him at this difficult time and for that I'll always be grateful. So we dusted off our very vague wedding plans.

We still didn't have a firm date in mind – or even a definite year. But what we did have was a venue. From the word go Lembit insisted on Powys Castle near Welshpool, bang in the heart of his constituency. It is a dramatic castle with a red hue, originally built for Welsh princes in around 1200. There are stunning Italianate gardens and long wide terraces that would be perfect for a summer wedding. It's a fairytale kind of place. Lembit thought *Hello!* would approve.

I had already been in touch with the castle's management to talk through the basics. Lembit and I had also visited so we could find out more in person. On arrival, the staff welcomed me like an old friend. Everyone had pulled out all the stops because they genuinely wanted to prove what a wonderful, romantic venue the castle could be. No wedding had ever been held there before so it was a big deal. It's a National Trust property so the charity's staff and volunteers would be involved and they were all fantastic. There was plenty of food for us to taste, amazing local cheeses that I knew Lembit would adore and whole ranges of organic goodies. It should have been a great day, but it wasn't.

'Where's Lembit?' The same old two words framed the day.

Weeks previously I had asked Lembit and his long-suffering secretary to protect this diary date. I was fully aware of how much the effort the castle staff would go to. Besides, it had taken me ages to get all involved in the same place at the same time. Stifyn, who was due to be our wedding organiser, was coming up from Cardiff and had postponed meetings to make sure he attended.

I had already known that Lembit had meetings in the morning so he wouldn't be able to be with us at the start of the day. But as usual he was late. When he did turn up, he was with his agent David Selby and wedding plans seemed very far from his mind. He was grumpy and distracted, just as he had been for the engagement photographs at Llangoed Hall. The staff and I tried to talk to him about the venue and the way the wedding could work but he seemed to be barely listening. It suddenly dawned on me why he was there: David had a camera. What he appeared to be concentrating on was a new photograph for his latest election leaflet. I assumed that I was to play the part of the doting, political wife-to-be.

I knew and liked David (he had, after all, stayed in Lembit's London flat for a while), but even I, polite as I am by instinct, found it difficult to fall in with this seemingly unilateral change of plan.

It seemed love had little to do with it. I had my photo taken with Lembit, and he gave Stifyn about 15 minutes of his time and then dashed down to London. Clearly there was something more important to attend to than his wedding plans, so off he went. Stifyn and I joined the staff for the sumptuous lunch they'd prepared and I tried to hide my embarrassment.

Then I took a call from Stifyn that afternoon that couldn't have been more to the point: 'Siân, I don't think this wedding is ever going to take place.' How right he was. On another occasion we went out to dinner in one of our favourite curry houses in Newtown. We had had a lot of laughs there over the years and so I was hoping we could rekindle some of those memories. But things went wrong again when I brought the subject around to the wedding.

We wouldn't have been able to invite more than 100 people to Powys Castle because the fire regulations were so strict. So we had discussed having two more parties to keep everyone happy: one in the constituency, the other at Westminster. Both would have had quite different flavours but having three events meant a huge amount of organisation and big budgets, all of which would land on my shoulders.

As our food arrived, I started to ask Lembit about guest lists, the food, the entertainment and all the other big issues. He didn't want to engage so I brought it back down to basics. Before I did anything, I needed a rough idea of how much we were prepared to spend. But money – or the lack thereof –- was always a wildly sensitive subject with Lembit. It was off limits.

'So, what do you think our budget should be?' I asked.

Lembit didn't reply. So I asked again – and again. As his non-answers mounted up and my question came again and again I felt like Jeremy Paxman in that infamous interview with Michael Howard. But I was a woman having dinner with her fiancé. I shouldn't be made to feel like Jeremy Paxman and he shouldn't act like a home secretary on the run.

Politics ultimately got in the way of our wedding – so as it turned out I owe a lot to Tony Blair for distracting us in 2005. The election had been called for 5 May and Lembit had a lot to deal with. I felt desperately sorry for him. His father had died just five days before so a spring or summer wedding was already out of the question. We very loosely discussed a winter date, though we were also ready to put the day off until 2006. Frankly, I couldn't have cared less. The whole thing seemed so unreal to me that the dates were entirely irrelevant.

The campaign was exciting, though. In the national polls, Labour had Iraq to contend with as well as a lot of question marks about Blair's leadership. In Lembit's constituency, local issues clearly dominated a lot of the campaigning. Lembit threw himself into the challenge. He joked that, whenever he went out knocking on doors, people always looked past him in case I was around the corner as well.

When he was re-elected in the 2005 election – on an increased majority – he was thrilled. 'I love you, I love you, I love you,' he repeated to me before one of the victory photo calls outside Welshpool Town Hall. But by now I was less likely to be fooled by this. By now I was starting to believe he loved winning even more.

If the election was the highpoint of Lembit's year, then the massive celebrations for ITV's 50th birthday were pretty much the professional highpoint of mine. I was pleased that I was still with ITV: I was by far the longest-standing female national weather presenter on the network. In an industry obsessed by youth, I seemed to have staying power, so there was no way I wanted to miss a single moment when ITV threw its big party.

The Queen was our big guest and every star from the worlds of entertainment, politics, business and sport would be vying to meet her. Lembit and I had been invited separately, but of course we planned to arrive together. I stress the word 'planned'. The idea was that the pair of us would share a car to the party with my friend Becky Mantin from our ITV weather team. I was first to be collected, then Becky leaped into the cab at her flat and we headed to Russell Square Tube Station to pick up Lembit. But he wasn't there.

Ten minutes passed, then 20, then 30. Fortunately, Becky and I always have plenty to talk about, so we were happy to gossip away as we waited. But after half an hour I knew we had to get serious. This was a royal reception. It was the biggest deal in ITV's year – and ITV was my main employer. I couldn't be late. I called Lembit's mobile one more time, but as usual the answering service kicked in.

Finally, he strode towards the car when we had been there 45 minutes. He had the old hangdog look on his face that never boded well for the rest of the evening. It was only much later that Becky gave me her take on the car journey. I was so immune to this kind of thing that I hadn't noticed. Lembit hadn't said as much as hello to either of us. That had seemed normal to me. He hadn't apologised for keeping us waiting. I hadn't expected him to. He hadn't even complimented either of us on what we were wearing – and for such a huge event we had both pulled out all the stops.

I was wearing a black Frank Usher evening dress with a

lime-green feather boa over my shoulders. Lembit, of all people, knew how much I loved clothes. But the only thing he commented on was my fake feather boa. Apparently, it was moulting over the car seat.

When our tense drive to the studios was over, we all climbed out of the car. I paid the bill, Becky offered half of it and Lembit simply disappeared towards the red carpet and the cameras. That's when his mood got worse.

It was celebrity soup that night. Absolutely everyone who is or was anyone was there. The banks of paparazzi were as big as they get. And it all worked in exactly the way it always does. They want photos of couples together, they want groups of colleagues or friends together. Then they want everyone to split up so they can get individual shots as well.

'Siân, over here, on your own.'

I followed the calls automatically. And I didn't for one moment think they wanted my picture because I looked so fabulous that night, moulting green feather boa or not. The reality is that the photographers always do. Who knows – you might get killed in a car crash or involved in a scandal – and they've got the most up-to-date final photo of you for the first editions – it's grim but it's show business. The only person who didn't seem to understand was Lembit. He furiously marched off into mêlée of the party proper.

Once we got past the photographers we were divided into two groups – those who would get to be in the same room as the Queen and those who would not. Everyone was then marshalled into separate groups, politicos in one area, news teams in another, sports people in another and so on. Lembit tried to tag on to my little group, but he was pulled away to join the other MPs. It was a fantastic opportunity to catch up with so many acquaintances you often miss because of conflicting schedules. I got to chat to Nicholas Owen, Trevor McDonald, Fern Britton, Philip Schofield and lots more of the ITV gang. But would I get to meet the Queen? Not every group, let alone every guest, would get a handshake – I think if we had done so then the party would have lasted all year. But as we all milled around it looked as if I was going to be one of the lucky ones. By now, I had met Prince Charles plenty of times, but the Queen was a first. I can't deny I was intrigued and excited. I was also pretty certain she wouldn't have the first clue who I was.

How wrong I was.

Not only did I talk to the Queen but I talked to her for longer than almost anyone else at the whole reception. Weather had been in the news that summer – the BBC was under fire for supposedly bringing in a new policy of accentuating the positives. Its forecasters were said to be focusing on sunshine rather than rain. The Queen was clearly following the story. She wanted my opinions and she picked my brains on the way we wrote our scripts and did our research.

As we talked, my old love of the absurd kept making me want to laugh. From the corner of my eye I could see Charles Allen, the chairman of ITV, hovering. Clearly, he was desperate to move the Queen on to his other far bigger and brighter stars. I had a feeling that the Queen would probably have no idea about the real big names like Ant and Dec or Chris Tarrant. But she did know her weather presenters and she was standing her ground. We talked a bit about Scotland and the way the weather changes on the hills. She was clearly an outdoor woman and she wanted to know more about the nitty-gritty of our forecasts. It also seemed as if climate change and the environment concerned her just as much as it did her eldest son. And all this was in the middle of the star-studded ITV party. The whole room seemed to be watching in amazement as our conversation went on and on.

When she finally moved on, I rejoined my colleagues with a huge smile on my face. It had all felt quite surreal. She was much shorter and warmer than I thought she would be. I could hardly believe it had happened. Then I rejoined Lembit and the other politicians. The fun wasn't over.

He was with Menzies Campbell, who I hadn't met before. It wasn't the smoothest of moments. 'So, when are you two finally going to get married?' Menzies asked Lembit, with just a hint more ice than I had expected.

Lembit didn't reply, so I tried to step into the breach with a weak joke. 'Roughly when ITV stops celebrating its 50th birthday,' I said.

The industry seemed to have been celebrating this landmark birthday forever! Menzies did laugh, very briefly. But he then made another comment, to the effect that our wedding would never happen.

Wow, old Menzies's a bit sharp! I remember thinking. I'd admired him so much for the anti-war stance he had taken two years earlier. And it seemed to me that he was quite prepared to take the piss out of Lembit.

GRIEF

I didn't see a lot of Lembit in the autumn of 2005. It's funny how two people who are supposed to be getting married can actually end up living very separate lives.

But it was strange to see so little of him. I had long since lost my battle of the diary. By now, I knew I would never be told where he was going or when. 'Information I did not need to know', perhaps Lembit felt. So, as the clocks went back on 2005 and extending into the summer of 2006, there seemed to be more and more nights when he didn't come home at all. There were more mornings when he wouldn't explain why. Just as draining was the fact that he no longer seemed to care about the inconsistencies of the stories he told me. Leaving parties appeared to be his default excuse for any absences. But just how many times would 'Emma' be leaving his office? How many drinks parties might he think she would require before she found pastures new?

Lembit's leftfield take on life had been one of the things that first attracted me to him, but by now his impulsive behaviour was definitely loosing its lustre for me. When you live too long in a dysfunctional relationship, your batteries, your standards and your resistance all get low. You start to accept unacceptable behaviour; you forget what ought to happen and how people should really behave.

That's where I was. I felt I had been buffeted by mood swings for too long. Suddenly that autumn I reached my tipping point. I realised I didn't want to marry Lembit. I didn't want to stay with him, but I didn't know what to do.

I knew there was a lot of baggage to sort out – and I don't just mean the boxes of women's shoes (old stock from his ladies' shoe shop) in the house in Wales. I was very aware that so many people wanted us to get married. Everywhere we went the public were so supportive of us. In the constituency, people still saw us as a golden couple. Weirdly enough, I felt I would be letting them down by admitting we had failed. Remember, I'm the good girl: I don't let people down.

I was just as bothered by the sense that I had failed. I hadn't managed to help Lembit fulfil his potential; I hadn't fixed or healed him. I hadn't even got him to remotely cut back on his drinking.

Unfortunately knowing I should leave was one thing but doing so quite another. I knew our split would get played out in public and I literally shuddered as I thought about all the calls we would get from reporters, all the gossip and innuendo that would seep into the coverage. I decided I would try to laugh it off as the curse of *Hello!* But I didn't expect it to be easy.

Nor was I relishing the idea of actually doing the deed and telling Lembit my plans. All my previous relationships had ended in a calm adult fashion. Both sides had always seen the writing on the wall and been prepared to help each other move on. Something told me Lembit would not go quietly, that he would make a drama out of this crisis. I had to pick my moment very carefully. But at least there was no rush. With Lembit and me hardly seeing each other and barely speaking there was no pressure.

I knew we could live together, apart, almost indefinitely. Through accident or design, I tended to be in Wales whenever he was in London and vice versa. By now, he was going off the radar for long periods. He went a whole week during party conference without getting in touch. He no longer attempted to tell me where he was, with whom, or what he was doing. We probably passed each other going up the M40 some nights. Just as well.

Everything changed one awful night that November. I had been to the National Theatre to see *Coram Boy*. It was an adaptation of Jamila Gavin's novel about the disparate lives of foundling children left at the Coram Hospital in 18th-century England. My old pal DG was the outgoing chairman of the Coram Foundation so I already had a lot of background to the subject. I had been looking forward to seeing the play for ages and it didn't disappoint.

In the cab home, I turned on my mobile and saw that I had a message from Lembit – that in itself was a surprise. We were barely speaking at that point. I wasn't expecting to see him at the flat that night nor did I expect him to call to say where he might be. The message was short and terrible.

'My brother's dead,' was pretty much all he said. But in those few words he sounded worse than I had ever heard him.

Straight away I called him. He was on a train up to Leicester – and he was crying.

I had met his younger brother Endel several times over the years. He was even taller than Lembit, some 6 foot 10, I think. And he was a Goth, so he wasn't someone you would easily forget. Like the rest of the family, apart from dear old Uno, he was a big drinker, but he was only in his late thirties, some three or four years younger than Lembit. He had been rushed to hospital with pancreas problems a few years previously, but I thought that was all over and done with. Endel was warned at the time to give up alcohol, otherwise he would be dead within a few years.

'Was it an accident?' I could only think it must have been a car crash. Surely it couldn't have been a shooting or some other terrible event? The death certificate said pneumonia – incredible for someone in his thirties.

'I'm coming up tonight,' I said as I looked out of the taxi window. I calculated I could be at his mother's home in Leicester just after midnight.

'No, don't. Just come for the funeral,' he told me.

So I did, and naturally the whole family were beside themselves. I really felt for them. First, they had lost Uno six months previously and now Endel was gone. The huge crowds of Goths, all suitably dressed in black, were equally distressed. Endel had died so young. His death would hit Lembit far harder than his father's – and already he was struggling to cope. Desperate to comfort him, I reached out for his hand in the middle of the funeral. But he pulled it away.

In the first few weeks after this latest funeral, I could tell how much Lembit was hurting, and how much he was bottling up inside. The fixer in me came back to the fore. More than ever, I could see a broken man who needed mending. I knew I had to be there for the days or nights when he was finally ready to talk.

As he tried to deal with his grief and his demons, I hit the shops to try to track down the most wonderful book. The American playwright Joan Dideon had written *The Year of Magical Thinking* as her response to the loss of her husband and the life-threatening illness of her daughter in the same year. I had found it incredibly moving and important, and I was convinced it would help Lembit. My friend Trish also pointed me towards some advice and information about bereavement on the BBC's website. Again, I told Lembit where it all was and even printed out whole sections for him. I'm not sure he ever looked at a single word.

What left him so badly damaged was that he hadn't just lost his dad and his brother that year. One of his closest friends, Graham Cowley, died in 2004 as well. Lembit had been planning to ask him to be his best man. He was a former colleague from Lembit's Procter & Gamble days and had helped out when a business venture of Lembit's almost went bankrupt. His death from cancer had hit Lembit hard: his whole year was marked by illness, funerals and tragedy.

So, less than a month after I had finally decided to leave Lembit, suddenly I felt obliged to stay.

Chapter Sixteen
Playing Games

How ironic that just when I had mentally given up on our relationship Lembit and I were suddenly asked to do a pair of major 'celebrity couple' television shows.

In the early days of 2006, we got calls from the producers of both *Who Wants to be a Millionaire* and *The Weakest Link* to see if we wanted to appear in their latest one-off celebrity programmes. But my heart was never going to be in the task. I knew I would feel a complete fraud sitting next to Lembit and pretending that all was well in our confused and unhappy little world.

But in the end I had to say yes. In particular, the special editions of *Millionaire* are hugely important to charities. They matter because you don't get many other chances to raise so much cash for your cause in such a short period of time. It's also a mention of your charity on primetime TV. Being able to hand over tens of thousands of pounds would be an incredible event. So I knew I had to agree.

Clearly, the shows weren't going to be a barrel of laughs for us as a couple. Warning bells had always gone off when we had shared the same stage in the past. Previously, Lembit and I had gone on *The Keith Barret Show* to be interviewed by its spoof host, played by Rob Brydon, a true comic genius.

'Wow, he's hard work!' Rob had said about Lembit on the programme. Somehow we managed to raise some laughs but it hadn't been easy and I was mortified my partner seemed so prickly in public.

Now, as we prepared to sit next to each other again in the high stools of *Millionaire*, I no longer cared how Lembit behaved or how we were perceived. Bearing in mind how the show turned out, that was just as well.

In January 2006, we arrived at the studios. We had been told to wear as much red as possible – of all things we were being filmed for the Valentine's Day special. I couldn't believe that in the dying days of our relationship we were being pitched as love's young dream. If only the producers had known.

As it turned out, we didn't need to be as loved-up as that. My old pals Laurence and Jackie Llewelyn-Bowen went on ahead of us and as they made it right up the million-pound mark they filled up the whole of the Valentine's Day programme. Lembit and I still recorded our slot that day in January but we got a stay of execution until Easter before the public saw how dysfunctional our relationship had become.

As was becoming normal for the pair of us, things were tense from the start. Lembit had been late arriving at the studios – *plus ça change* – so he only caught the end of the rehearsal and that may well have made the experience even more nerve-wracking. What made it worse was the deflation that we and everyone else experienced when Laurence and Jackie got to the magic million-pound question.

We were all watching from the green room, as rapt as everyone else.

After answering some 14 questions, the couple were holding a cheque for £500,000. Jackie had told me earlier that this was their dream payout. They were raising funds for a small charity: the Shooting Star children's hospice in Hampton, Southwest London. Half a million pounds would make an incredible difference to its work, but a million pounds would help even more. So Laurence and Jackie decided to go for it and play the final question.

'Translated from the Latin, what is the motto of the United States?' was the million-pound question.

I didn't even need to think back to my A-level Latin. When Laurence picked 'In God We Trust', I was convinced he was right.

But he wasn't. The computer came up with a different answer: 'Out of Many, One'.

Laurence and Jackie saw their payout fall from £500,000 to just £32,000.

They were distraught – Jackie was crying as she rejoined us in the green room. Weeks later the producers announced that the couple's final question had been ambiguous and allowed them to film a new million-pound question. This time around, they passed on it so managed to take away £500,000 for their charity.

But we knew nothing about this on our cold January day

when Lembit and I finally walked into the studio to film our show. All we felt was the utter deflation of everyone in the building. It had been a stark reminder of how high the stakes on the game really were.

Chris's introduction made us sound like a charmed couple – and it raised a lot of laughs in the studio. 'The pair first met five years ago when Lembit was the Lib Dem spokesman for Wales and is said to have wooed Siân with endless games of chess and long romantic conversations about his favourite subject – the earth being hit by asteroids. Despite this, Siân has gone on record saying Lembit is the most fascinating man she has ever met.'

I smiled broadly. They really had been light and innocent days. Chris was laughing at us, but I thought it sounded sweet. Back then, we had been really happy. It was a shame that we would never see those days again.

After the initial chit-chat came what felt like the most important part of the show: the chance to explain a little about your chosen charity. It is a vital showcase. A single minute on prime-time television can have a huge impact on a charity's profile and fundraising abilities. I had chosen NCH and I knew that Vivien Fowle, the celebrity co-ordinator, was watching from the wings with fingers and toes tightly crossed. I didn't want to let her down. So, I took a deep breath. I must have spent thousands of hours in front of the cameras by this point in my career but I don't think I had ever felt so nervous. In the end, I think I said exactly what I wanted. I mentioned the huge variety of work NCH does, the vastly different types of children and families it helps and the ongoing importance of the work it does.

Then it was Lembit's turn. In honour of his father, he

had chosen the Motor Neurone Disease Association. He too had less than a minute to get his reasons across and his words clearly came from the heart. He said a little about how the illness hits people, he talked about the charity and then ended on a conviction that a cure could – and would – be found. It was powerful stuff.

The charity mentions out of the way, Chris started a bit more banter about the way we planned to play the game. I had met him a few times before. I liked him, back then.

'Which one of you is the decisive one?' Chris asked. 'I know Siân quite well, but I can't really work you two out.'

Lembit decided to reply. 'We pretend to defer to the other person but at the end of the day, once one person has made the decision, the other one is duty bound to argue about it,' he said.

What the hell did that mean? I thought, trying to keep smiling. I had feared Lembit would be a difficult partner on the show, but I hadn't expected things to go downhill before we even got to our first question. When Chris asked Lembit if I was romantic and he replied that I could be 'when she switches it on', I was horrified. How cynical did that sound? It was cruel, as well as untrue.

'By now a few warning bells had gone off,' I told a friend afterwards, when we discussed the show.

'Warning bells? More like distress flares!' he replied.

Fortunately, Lembit and I won plenty of laughs when the show finally got going. Our first question was to complete the funny quotation: 'Why did the chicken...?' so we would have looked pretty foolish to have fallen at such an early hurdle. We made it to £300 with no lifelines used, no problems and a few laughs.

Then Lembit became very weird.

Our fourth question needed us to do some counting. We had to work out how many of the signs of the zodiac have names beginning with the letter 'L'. I knew the moment Chris asked this that we were in trouble. Lembit is into astronomy, not astrology, and doesn't know much about horoscopes and star signs.

'This is sky stuff, you should know it,' Lembit told me, slightly more fiercely than strictly necessary.

So we started to try to count up as many star signs as we could remember.

Halfway through the count Lembit told me off, in a half-joking way. Apparently, I was using the wrong fingers for the count. I leaned over to touch his leg as I chided him about it and then he said it.

'Don't touch me!'

I must admit that at the time I didn't even notice that he said it. For me this kind of comment was par for the course, the kind of thing he might say when he was trying to be funny. I was also so immune to his offbeat reactions to things that I didn't flinch or see it as particularly newsworthy. By this time, I was past caring about his moods and comments. If only I had known how the public would respond...

Anyway, we made it through the next set of questions before Lembit once more went into passive aggressive mode. We had a question about women's gymnastics and I was pretty sure I knew the answer.

'Are you sure?' Lembit asked me. 'I'm not taking responsibility for this. If you are absolutely sure and take absolute and full responsibility, I'll agree with you,' he said.

I laughed but inside I was furious. The only reason for us being on the show was to raise money for charity and both of us genuinely believed in the causes we were supporting. Surely we should be working together to ensure we got them as much cash as possible?

I am embarrassed to say this, but the more Lembit questioned me, the more confidence I lost. It was as if I was being grilled at *Question Time*. 'But I'm not an opposition MP, I'm still meant to be your fiancée and we're in this together,' I wanted to whisper.

Once more it felt as if life with Lembit had become a competition. Maybe MPs are genetically programmed to see everything as a popularity contest; perhaps they can only measure things in terms of winners and losers. I don't think Lembit was playing *Millionaire* against the computer, I think he was playing against me. In his mind, I had got ahead by knowing most of the early questions, so now I had to be undermined.

I don't want to go through all the rest of the questions and the remainder of Lembit's increasingly difficult responses, but I was well aware he was acting like a spoiled child. Now I couldn't have cared less. The gulf between us could hardly have been wider.

At £32,000 we got the chance to mention our charities again.

'This buys two vans for disabled children at NCH,' I said.

'For motor neurone disease that's the kind of money that can begin to help find a cure,' said Lembit. And on we went.

We got to £64,000 and while I was certain I knew the answer to that question – who had written the novel *Saturday Night and Sunday Morning*? – I couldn't get the message across. Lembit's criticisms and cross-examinations had knocked my confidence for six. That evening he would have made me doubt my own name. We decided to take the money – but after we had the cheque Chris clicked his screen to reveal I had been right all along.

'Oh, Siân!' Lembit groaned, seeming to blame me for letting the opportunity pass.

I'm glad to say Chris picked him up on this straight away. I was glad of his support back then.

'Oh, Lembit!' he joked, in the same theatrical voice.

The moment filming stopped Lembit turned his mobile back on. We had our photos taken – all smiles – with Chris holding a big cheque. Then we went for drinks with the production crew. But that night not even Lembit felt like a drink.

'Shall we just go home?' I asked.

He nodded.

I was kicking myself all the way home from Elstree. We should have gone for it, I kept thinking. Interestingly enough, Lembit was thinking the opposite. 'I think we can hold our heads up proudly,' he said, as we headed up to my flat.

In those words I saw yet another crucial difference between us; another reason why our days were so clearly numbered. Like many politicians, Lembit lives in the present and for the future: he is not reflective. But I think we need to value the past. I believe that if you don't think about what has happened to you – and learn from it – you can never improve as a person. It meant that the Lembit next to me now was the way he would probably always be. And that wasn't good enough for me.

Anyway, it turned out we couldn't really hold our heads up proudly when the show was finally broadcast. Our body language and Lembit's criticisms were roundly condemned in the press and clearly struck a nerve with the public. One paper even set up a special website for people to post comments. It wouldn't have made easy reading for Lembit, which is probably why he never bothered.

A couple of weeks after the show aired we were on holiday in Majorca on behalf of the Great Ormond Street Hospital. So many expats came up to us to say how upset they were at Lembit's behaviour on *Millionaire*. And so many more came up to me when I was on my own to say what a fool my boyfriend was. Everyone seemed to remember the 'Don't touch me' comment. They all agreed I had been undermined.

'You deserve better, love,' one bruiser of a man told me.

All I could do was give a tense smile and move on. I wanted to exclaim that I knew the man was right, but that he didn't know how hard it was for me to leave.

Ironically enough, we had another 'couples' edition' of a game show to play in that year; another bit of acting for me now my mind was firmly elsewhere. This time it was for *The Weakest Link*. Again, we both agreed to the invitation because it was such an easy way to raise big money for charity.

The show is filmed in Pinewood and I was doing the weather at ITN in central London until late afternoon so I had an extra adventure in my day. The production team were worried I would get held up in traffic if I got an ordinary cab and so they sent one of the new taxi bikes to collect me. You get a helmet and a set of leathers to wear, then you cling on to your driver for dear life and weave your way through the rush hour. It was one of the most exciting and sometimes terrifying experiences of my year. And it helped me relax when I got to the studio. If I had survived that journey, then I would certainly survive a tongue-lashing from Anne Robinson!

As it turned out, Lembit and I gelled pretty well on that show. We smiled at each other and supported each other. But then we weren't on the podium for long. We were voted off early by the other competitors because they reckoned we were likely to be the most intelligent of the bunch. I was delighted. Just as with *I'm a Celebrity*, I'd got away with it! And we never got to pierce Anne's armour. She really does maintain the myth throughout. She joins everyone for a photo call before you start. She sneers, but says nothing. The Queen of Mean role fits her like a glove. Lembit availed himself of the complimentary drink in the Green Room afterwards and it took me forever to get him out of there.

Looking back, I feel as if I spent most of 2005 and 2006 living in limbo. My relationship was on borrowed time but I couldn't do the deed and finish it. I needed a Lady Macbeth in my life, someone to tell me to screw my courage to the sticking point and face up to the inevitable. Almost all my friends tried, but still I failed to hear.

What made it harder was that Lembit could still show flashes of the good guy of old. Just when I wanted to admit I couldn't take it any more, he would pull some nice trick out of the bag. A gentleman one day, a nightmare the next. Infuriating at times, exhilarating at others. Deliberate or not, this continued to buy him time. I was always happy to coast along when he was Dr Jekyll – it made up for the other times when he was Mr Hyde. And so the months passed.

We all enjoyed his good side for the first part of my parents' 50th wedding anniversary in the summer of 2006. I had planned a big party at our country house and pulled out all the stops to make it special for them. I cooked food on a gold theme and sprinkled some dishes with gold leaf to make it suit the occasion. Lembit flew down to Swansea to pick up my parents in his plane and bring them back to Welshpool. And, while he did have to leave halfway through the afternoon to go to a summer fête in the constituency, he was on good form while he was with us. This was Dr Jekyll.

Soon afterwards, Mr Hyde resurfaced, just as he always did. And I was glad, looking back, because the more often I saw this side, the less pain I would feel when I finally picked the moment to leave.

The bad incident came in August of that year when a gang of friends arrived for a big get-together in mid-Wales. For some reason Lembit was at his most petulant, so no one was having a lot of fun. Eric and Trish were with us for several days and said Lembit was unrecognisable from the livewire they had first met in the Camden tapas bar a few years previously. Mind you, so was I – we must have been like *Who's Afraid of Virginia Woolf?* played out in front of their eyes. Eric also told me something very strange about the weekend. Apparently, Lembit had cornered him for a very long, very odd conversation about relationships – and the end thereof. At one point, he told Eric that he was 'concerned about the way it would play in the press'.

At the time I couldn't understand what he might mean because at that point we were still a couple – we had taken no steps towards ending the relationship. Even if we had, why would a simple split between consenting adults play badly in the press? Couples break up all the time. If no one else is involved and everything is amicable, what's to play badly?

So was there someone else involved? I wondered if the curse of the Libido Dems was about to strike again.

Journalists and friends in politics have finally told me a few secrets. One of them was about the Cheeky Girls during the time of the Bromley and Chislehurst by-election in the summer of 2006 – just before our house party in Wales. The election had been a huge test for the Lib Dems. They had been trying to overcome the Conservatives in one of the safest Tory seats in the Home Counties and had only fallen short by some 600 votes. Ben Abbotts, the Lib Dem hopeful, had been photographed with a Cheeky Girl on each arm as part of the campaign. It seemed completely bizarre. Was their new publicity campaign a good career move?

In honour of Lembit's dad, I had agreed that my next big trek would raise money for the Motor Neurone Disease Association. All the usual suspects signed up for the adventure alongside me. In the late summer of 2006, we were to traverse Mont Blanc.

Before we went, we had some serious training to do, however. Mont Blanc rises up to some 4,800 metres above sea level. People die on it, so the trek was never going to be some cliché walk in the park. We also wanted to raise more money than ever before and so we did more than just sign people up for sponsorship: Novello hosted a big fundraising night at the Royal Surrey Golf Club to give our efforts a kick-start. We also had a great auction – I offered myself up for a 'day on the weather' and was 'bought' by Marlene, a lovely generous lady who shadowed me at ITN for a shift and has now become a friend.

We flew to Chamonix, collected our kit and headed up into the mountains. From the first steps, my mind was clear – it always is when I go on a hike. Everything gets placed in perspective and nothing matters as much as it does at home. All I want to do when I walk is to enjoy every moment – and in France that was never going to be a problem. The trails were tough so we needed some hearty food to keep us going, and we got it. There was lots of country bread with cheese and saucissons, plenty of raclettes and some incredible picnics. We had great French guides – they were fit as fiddles even though they smoked from dawn till dusk and could only ever see the mountains through a fog of thick cigarette smoke!

Thankfully, we weren't camping on this trip. We stayed in some basic little hostels in the mountains and it was first come, first served when it came to the rooms. After we wised up to this, we would literally run the last stretch each night to get to the hotels first and try to bag somewhere with its own shower and a bit of privacy.

At the end of the trip, Lembit made one of his grand gestures. He flew in to Geneva with a businessman supporter and the head fundraiser for the MND Association in order to meet us at the end of the trek the next day. And he was on good form – even though the three of them had been out on the town in Chamonix the night before. But to give him credit he wasn't as loopy as usual and for once seemed genuinely interested in how we had all done. As we always did on the last night of a trek, we had a big communal meal. We made speeches and vowed to do it all again very soon.

But travel proved to be the final swan song: our last hurrah as a couple would be played out in paradise. I had been chosen to do a trip to Fiji for a travel-writing assignment and for Lembit this was a hugely significant destination. His late father had been offered a job at the university there and as a boy Lembit had been obsessed with the islands. After such a terrible year, I thought he deserved the chance to see them in style: perhaps the resonance they had with his father might give him the chance to lay some demons to rest.

We stayed in some wonderfully upmarket island resorts: white sands, lavish rooms, wonderful food and service. I'm not a big beach person – I can't sit still long enough. But I did get to relax in Fiji and, as if you wouldn't know it, Lembit and I enjoyed ourselves. It truly is paradise and, like Wales, the land of song and rugby.

But by now I had hardened my heart and I was wise to the way the ups and downs of dating Lembit worked. A few good times in paradise would no longer be enough to keep us together through all the usual frustrations at home. More than a year had passed since his best friend and father had died; nearly a year had passed since the death of his brother. If I had been able to heal him, then I would have done so by now. And if I couldn't – because he didn't want me to – then finally it was time to move on.

This time there could be no more excuses.

Lembit had less holiday time than I did, so he arranged to fly home from Fiji. My travel-writing gig gave me the chance to fly on out to New Zealand for an extra week.

Nothing was said as he headed off for his flight, but there was something intensely moving about the way we parted. I was staying on for an extra night and had gone down to the beach to see him off. The hotel staff put garlands around Lembit's neck. Everyone was smiling and there was music in the air as he boarded the boat to the island's airport. This could be the last time I see him, I thought, out of nowhere. We were in paradise. It was so romantic, but suddenly so sad. So hot, but so cold. I saw him fade into the distance. His discarded red garland bobbed on the water. Lembit looked sad, and I felt like crying.

New Zealand cured my heartache and I had the most wonderful trip. I was on my own and I had never felt better. From the moment my plane left Fiji, I felt this rush of liberation.

My whole trip had been arranged down to the final detail. I was on the go the whole time, criss-crossing the islands and seeing a huge number of its most wonderful sights. It all went like a dream. If I ever live anywhere other than this country, I think it could only be New Zealand.

I loved the sea, the food, the wines, the mountains... But perhaps more importantly, I loved the people. The Kiwis had such big open hearts. They were always ready to give something a try, to face some new challenge; they were optimistic, loved the outdoors, appreciated good cooking and loved rugby. What's not to like?

Did I miss Lembit? Not for one second! I've never minded travelling on my own. Going on that first charity trek to the Himalayas proved that. And back then, in 2006, I needed time to think. Lembit had gone bereavement crazy, or so I thought. I had been grieving for our relationship and now it was time for me to snap out of it.

In the Cloudy Bay vineyard at the tip of the South Island I watched the sun set –the same stunning sunset that was on the label of the wine bottle that was on my table. I went to the beach where they filmed *The Piano*, I landed in a ski-plane on a glacier of Mount Cook and I even got a marriage proposal!

I had been flown up by helicopter to a patch of the highest privately owned land in the country. It was breathtakingly beautiful. And, while I walked around, the land's bachelor owner very pointedly told me how much he wanted a wife. On our way back down the mountain, I couldn't stop smiling. Clearly it had been a joke, but hadn't it also been a Lembit-style proposal about a proposal? At least I was wise to all this now.

My stay in New Zealand lasted just over a week but it changed me. It was the first time I had been alone since making my mind up about Lembit – and it had been all the better because of my solitude. Every day had been calm and uplifting. I had been able to sip a glass of New Zealand Sauvignon Blanc in the evening and then get up early the next morning to go biking or walking. It was wonderful not to be with someone who would have a few drinks and start an argument over nothing.

Over the week, I went thought the motions and sent Lembit a few texts, but got very few replies. He didn't meet me at the airport when I got home and we hadn't arranged any romantic reunion dinner. Certainly there was no carpet of candles waiting for me at my flat. Lembit was off the radar – and I didn't care.

Within weeks, I received the most awful phone call from Wales: my dad was in hospital. That was when I rushed home and everything, finally, became clear. I saw how precious life is; how fast it passes. And how much time we can waste if we stay too long with the wrong person. That was when I made my call and ended our relationship; that was when I became free again.

Chapter Seventeen
Saying Goodbye

We met in a pub in Camden. It's a warm, slightly bo-ho place with good food and a nice North London crowd. It was neutral territory for both of us.

Lembit needs a good meal. I can't believe it, but those were pretty much my first thoughts when he walked into the pub. I was so used to mothering him and trying to fix him that I couldn't stop myself even then. He always ate so intermittently, if at all. But that day he looked even more gaunt than normal. I bet he hasn't eaten all day, I thought. But then I kicked myself. He is a 41-year-old politician; he is no longer your problem and he should never have been your problem in the first place – that's the whole point of this meeting.

We got down to business pretty much straight away. Why waste time on small talk when you might never see one another again? We talked about our properties, our possessions, the press... It was cold and calm. I felt absolutely nothing for the man in front of me; it was as if I was talking to a stranger. And funnily enough he did look very different. It wasn't just the deeper shadows on his face and the dark rings around his eyes: he was dressed differently. He was wearing an absurdly trendy shirt and new glasses, and he wasn't wearing a tie.

I have always admired the way the likes of Jeremy Vine dress. I felt the relaxed, weekend look Jeremy has on his *Politics Show* would give Lembit a real lift as well. So over the years, I had bought him plenty of shirts, jackets and trousers that would provide the same relaxed style. But Lembit never quite got it. If he wore the clothes, he would always put on a tie, even a stained one, though his whole look cried out to be open-necked.

That evening in the pub he had finally come round to the modern way of thinking, but clearly he had done it for her, not for me. Perhaps he'd begun feeling his age, trying to shave a few years off by dressing down. I suspected it might take a bit more than that, but I had to admire him for trying.

As we sat there I remembered clearly where and when I had bought the suit he had on. But he was welcome to it. He would need more than a good wardrobe to rebrand himself. He seemed soulless that night. I have always loved a man's eyes, but his seemed darker and smaller now. This new girl was welcome to him.

She was certainly on his mind. He took texts and calls from her all evening. He was heading off to see her afterwards, he said. So his supposedly youthful new look was indeed aimed at her. For some reason I felt I should wish her luck. God knows she was going to need it.

SAYING GOODBYE

As usual, I picked up the bill and we left the pub together. But, while Lembit wasn't spending money on me, he wasn't quite the skinflint of old. As we said our formal goodbyes in Arlington Road, he flagged down a taxi rather than heading for the tube. I don't think I had ever seen him do that on his own before. How times had changed! He was such an inveterate bus getter rather than a cab hailer when we were together. As the taxi sped away, I couldn't help but remember the time he came to take me home from University College Hospital.

A couple of days later we had what would turn out to be our final phone conversation. We had to speak to tie up some more loose ends about the property we owned together in Wales. 'It'll be signed sealed and delivered within a month,' he snapped. I didn't think the legal and property world worked as fast as Lembit may have liked, yet nearly a year later I was still fielding calls from solicitors with the end of the saga some way off. Briefly in 2007 Lembit held the business and enterprise brief for the Lib Dems. Hopefully, he has more experience now about how it all works; hopefully, he's now sorted out his own finances.

Our final conversation was cold and my last words were final.

'I don't want to speak to you again and I think that we won't. I always thought that the two things that would ruin our relationship would be women and alcohol.' Then I hung up. More or less, those remain the last words I have said to him. I stand by them.

Some of Lembit's next words would not be quite so dignified. Like many others I sat in horror when I heard the comment he made in the House of Commons during

Prime Minister's Questions the following January. The house had roared with laughter as he stood up to ask a question about funding for Motor Neurone Disease. MPs really can be like children at times like this. But Lembit seemed to relish it. He loved being the centre of attention and all eyes were certainly on him that day.

'Not wishing to be cheeky, I thank the House for being so happy that I am so lucky. I should point out that the other sister is still single.'

He then tried to make his comment about funding for research into Motor Neurone Disease. But who remembers that? I thought it was a bit tacky, though he obviously thought it was appropriate and also funny. Obviously, I knew the staff at MND Association well. I guessed they would be mortified their message had been lost amid the furore of that comment. But it seemed I might have guessed wrong.

On 7 February 2007, I was due at a Downing Street reception with Tony and Cherie. It was sponsored by the MND Association and my trekking gang's big fundraising efforts on Mont Blanc and at Novello's golf-club evenings were due to be recognised as part of the evening. But where was my invitation? I had been asked to come, but had not yet been sent the vital paperwork to get through Downing Street's security. I made some calls and discovered a mystery: I was off the list, but no one would say exactly why.

Reading between the lines I had to assume the organisers felt Lembit and I were either/or guests and that they had to take sides so they picked him. So I was frozen out. The shock hit me far more than almost anything else about the break-up did. It was like a kick in the teeth and it seemed incredibly unfair.

Funnily enough, Novello's invitation still stood. She asked me if she should go.

'Absolutely, yes,' I told her. 'You raised thousands of pounds at your golf club for this charity. You deserve to be there.'

So Novello went and acted like a true friend throughout. Every time she spoke to one of the charity sponsors, she mentioned my name and the money my gang and I had raised. 'I'm here because of Siân,' she told all the organisers pointedly. She said the same to Cherie Blair, who ultimately made a fabulous comment of her own.

Some brief speeches were made to give the evening a focus. In one of them, the organiser gave a vote of thanks to Lembit.

'And we all know about Lembit,' said Cherie, rolling her eyes and effectively reminding everyone of his former Cheeky Girl comments.

Novello says Lembit's blush had to be seen to be believed. Certainly, I felt better after hearing the story – and I respect Cherie even more for having the guts to say what most people were thinking. But being excluded from Downing Street had really hurt and the rejection had touched another raw nerve.

Just before our split, I had gone back to mid-Wales and found a stack of letters and invitations forwarded to Lembit from his constituency office. A lot of people often wrote to me care of Lembit. Fool that I was, I had assumed he would pass anything on to me. He hadn't, and many of the out-of-date letters I found had clearly required a response.

The first that I picked up had been an official invitation to the President's Lunch at the Royal Welsh Show; the second had come from a four-year-old boy who wanted me to come to his birthday party; the third a wedding invite. And so the list went on. None of these letters had reached me so I hadn't been able to send my apologies, let alone turn up. And I was very upset. This was my professional and personal reputation that Lembit was playing with. I'm a stickler for thank-you cards and RSVPs.

'Why didn't you pass them on? Why, *why*?' I had asked Lembit.

But he refused to answer or even attempt an explanation. Information is control.

Having seen us together, my friend Jane Ashley rather grandly compared us to Charles and Diana in the early days of their marriage when everyone said he considered himself marginalised by his wife's popularity. I'm not so sure about that, or that Lembit felt that way.

Going through all those out-of-date letters and invitations, I then found something even more annoying. There was a 'congratulations on your engagement' card from Eleanor Burnham, the Lib Dem Assembly Member for North Wales. And it wasn't just any card; she had clearly gone to a huge amount of trouble to personalise it. It had a specially commissioned picture of planes and clouds, streaks of lightning and colourful umbrellas and all the other symbols that she associated with the pair of us. It was beautiful and so thoughtful. And as I held it in the summer of 2006 I suddenly remembered the time I had seen Eleanor back in 2004 after the engagement had been announced. We had been at the International Eisteddfod in Llangollen and she had asked if I liked the card.

'Yes, it was lovely. Thanks so much,' I had said, fibbing in order to protect Lembit because, like so many other things, I had never seen it. I then moved the conversation on. Eleanor must have thought I was the most lukewarm woman in Wales, I thought, after finally seeing this extra-special card. I'm amazed she ever spoke to me again.

Back to the days immediately after news of our split had broken. Suddenly the world seemed to have gone mad. I couldn't believe it triggered such ferocious media attention. Ironically enough, I found the publicity and the press interest far worse than the split itself.

But I didn't want people to worry about me because I was OK. I was never the victim that I think a lot of the columnists portrayed me to be – I had long since accepted that my relationship with Lembit was over. I am a public figure, but a private person and I have extraordinary friends who would see me though those storms.

But I couldn't ignore the realities of the news cycle. I was told that the Cheeky Girl was about to go public in the *News of the World* with the 'inside story' of how and when she and Lembit met. Somehow I didn't imagine any of it would make pleasant reading. Everyone I spoke to said I should once and for all give my side of the story. The *Mail on Sunday* offered me that chance. Throughout the interview, I remember sitting so still. I chose my words so carefully – I was so determined to retain my dignity and my composure. In a strange sort of way, I wanted to retain my privacy. But this was uncharted territory for me. It was the most personal interview I had ever given. Whenever I had spoken to the press before, it was about my work, the weather, a charity or a new programme. How would the reporters treat the story of my life?

I was told my story would be in the paper on the same day as the Cheeky Girl spilled her beans in the *News of the World*. In the last few days of that week, I was too worried to eat – and as my friends will attest I never stop eating! I didn't want the *Mail* to portray me as a victim, a wronged woman or a bitter old shrew. I am sure that, had they wanted to, they could have taken any line at all. In the end, to my huge relief, they simply told the story as it was.

But it was quite a different story in the *News of the World*. I was staggered, floored, by the interview it published with Gabriela. The sexual detail was just ghastly. Despite everything, some part of me still wanted to protect Lembit. I was mortified on his behalf – I knew how dangerous and damaging such an awful story would be in rural Wales. His constituents would be appalled; it could break his career. Her mother also had a lot to say on the relationship, which, again, I thought of as potentially very embarrassing to his career.

One final story does stick out in my memory from the last days of 2006 – or at least the pictures illustrating it stand out. As , I barely looked at the words. It was in the *Telegraph*, I think; the text balanced out by two large photographs. One was of Lembit and me in our all-weather gear, halfway up a mountain and in the middle of a wonderful hike. The other picture was of Lembit and the popster, all dolled up for an evening on the town. All my good memories of Lembit were wrapped up in that first version of him – the new girl was welcome to the second one.

Chapter Eighteen
New Starts

It wasn't over, for in the run-up to Christmas 2006. I heard a fresh set of disturbing stories from mid-Wales. It seemed Lembit had taken both the Cheeky Girls out on market day on to the streets of Newtown in the heart of his constituency. He probably imagined that being seen with them would make him seem young and cool, and win him the youth vote. Local friends say the kids were certainly out in force taking pictures on their mobile phones and laughing. When I was in town over New Year, I found out what some of the older generation – the backbone of the town and Lembit's real constituency – really thought.

'I wish I had hit him over the head with my handbag,' one wonderful and redoubtable older lady told me with passion.

'I wish you had too,' I whispered in her ear.

Old gentlemen in the town were just as kind to me. Many gruff farmers put their arms around me in the street and told me in no uncertain terms what they thought of their MP. I was sent flowers and deluged with messages of support and goodwill. I have never lost my faith in human nature, but, if I had, then the people of mid-Wales would have restored it.

That Christmas I did the weather at ITN in London but that's nowhere near as sad or lonely as it sounds. We're a great gang anyway, but at Christmas there's an even better sense of camaraderie in the office. That's why I've worked so many of the Christmas shifts over the years. And, since I don't have children of my own, I feel it's no great hardship for me to work the Christmas period.

With all the publicity over Lembit, I was very aware that people would probably be looking at me even more closely than normal that Christmas. The truth was I was feeling on top of the world; I was positively sparkling. Well, that was until my final shift ended on Boxing Day and I headed north up the M40 to mid-Wales. I was going to my refuge in the country and I was in for a shock.

The moment I unlocked the door on Boxing Day night – though I may well be wrong – I suspected they had all been there. Muddy paw prints from a big dog were all over my carpets. More than that, there was something different about the whole atmosphere of the house. I'm not a particularly spiritual person but something felt wrong.

I remember years earlier when Mark and I had got back to our house in Wiltshire to find we had been burgled. You feel violated and damaged by events like that. I had the same feeling that Boxing Day.

And it was truly my place. It was the one home in my life that I had put together from scratch; my heart and soul had gone into it. I hadn't scrimped on anything; I made no compromises. We had the most wonderful Melin Tregwynt Welsh throws, handmade oak furniture, carefully chosen objects. And we had enjoyed some great times there.

That Boxing Day evening I felt cold. It was the first time since the split that I really caught my breath; the first time I felt upset and vulnerable.

I strode around my house, forcing myself to snap out of it. And I did, because I knew I was in a better place than all three of them – all four, if you include their omnipresent mother.

New Year's Eve is the obvious time for fresh starts and New Year's Eve 2006 was to be the most positive of my life. My lesson to every woman – and every man – is to invest in your friends. Mine are invaluable; they are absolutely the best of the best. I am blessed by knowing them.

And that New Year's Eve a whole big gang of us were together to toast a bright new start. The cottage was full of fun and laughter. We had curry and champagne, and we talked and laughed as the clock made its way to midnight.

As I looked up into the Welsh night sky at one point in the evening, I thought how much happier this was than any of the New Year's Eves I had spent with Lembit. Walking through my kitchen later that night I got a flashback to the one New Year's Eve when I had gone to bed alone while Lembit and David Hamer sat downstairs. They had begun a game of chess over the kitchen table in the early hours. When I came down the next morning, I found them both asleep over the table.

Then there had been the New Year's Eve Lembit had got

himself into some kind of mysterious trouble. We had agreed to go to a New Year's Day party at Stifyn's in West Wales, but the night before Lembit had come home battered and bruised.

'Are you OK? What's happened?'

I wanted to help, but felt brushed aside.

All Lembit would say was that he had been beaten up. He said something about an alleyway; that it had happened so fast he hadn't known who had done it or what was going on.

Lembit went into lock-down. I couldn't get another word on the subject from him. Nor could anyone else at the New Year's lunch the next day, where his injuries were a talking point and his sullen stance drew a dark cloud over what should have been a happy gathering.

I thanked my lucky stars I was never going back to that.

On the first day of 2007, Jane Ashley and I headed out to hike a part of the Severn Way. It was a glorious start to a year that would continue to get better.

Back in London and back on the weather, I started to get thrown some wonderful compliments. I felt brighter, and funnily enough lots of people thought I was blonder! The papers said I had clearly decided to change my image in the post-Lembit world. In fact, I had been blonde for nearly a year. But maybe the change shone through only now that I had things to smile about. Every part of my day felt better now that I didn't have Lembit's dead weight dragging me down. No more battles about his diary and his drinking; no more worries about his whereabouts. I could go to receptions at six and leave by eight. I wouldn't be woken up at 2am by a key turning in my front door. It was wonderful.

The relief meant I could even laugh at some of the ridiculous stories that were still being printed in the papers. Early in the year, we had a classic. An extraordinary interview appeared in one of the newspapers in the middle of January. Sources close to Lembit said Stifyn was a Camilla-style 'third person' in what had apparently been a very crowded relationship. The article said I took Stifyn's calls 'at all hours of the day and night', that we spent weekends at each other's homes and that we went to parties together. As charge sheets go, it wasn't exactly going to get me locked up. But it was also a load of lies. Sadly, I rarely saw him during the Lembit years. For some reason, Lembit felt threatened by him. Stifyn has very sensitive antennae about people. He once said about Lembit, 'There's something about him I don't quite believe.'

Like I say, I did manage to laugh about this sort of thing in the end. But at the time I was upset that a dear friend – and a very strong friendship – had been brought into the media war. I hated that Stifyn then started to get calls from the press asking for his side of the story; I also felt for his partner David. Lembit probably hated this too, but that's a story I don't feel I want to repeat here. My feeling then – and now – was that I should move on.

Of all things *Hello!* magazine helped me do so. Its legendary fixer, the Marquesa de Varela, had been in touch to see if I wanted to do a big interview about my new life as a happy single woman. I agreed straight away – I wanted to prove that you don't need to have a man or be in a couple to live life to the full.

What I didn't know was that the magazine had also been

in touch with Lembit. He and the popster did an interview and shoot for the same issue.

I did my interview and pictures at the Goring Hotel in London. It seemed safe neutral territory. But Lembit wasn't so sensitive: he picked the Lake Vyrnwy Hotel in his constituency in mid-Wales. It is a place we had been to lots of times as a couple; a place that means a lot to me – somewhere I often go to with friends and where I know some of the staff. We often cycled round the lake and then go on to the hotel for tea. I thought it was wrong that Lembit was taking the girl there. It turned out I wasn't alone.

'None of us can believe he's bringing her here,' said a waitress, after the photo-shoot. 'We all think he's got a hell of a cheek!'

But what made everyone in the hotel laugh – except perhaps Lembit – was that he didn't just bring the one Cheeky Girl. The other sister and the mother rolled up as well. They both made their way into a fair few of the photographs.

Lembit also had a tough ride in the interview. Peter Robertson asked about the claims that he had intervened over threats to deport the sisters. A Lib Dem spokesman stated that Lembit hadn't lobbied anyone and had acted perfectly properly in referring the matter to the appropriate MP. Peter also dug into the exact chronology of the relationship. Lembit has always set great store by saying it only began after we had split. It doesn't actually bother me either way.

Ingrid Tarrant and I had some real heart-to-hearts that spring. How strange that one of my friends should see her marriage implode just before my relationship ended! We both tried to support each other through the worst of it. After many long talks, we concluded that we had wasted too many years on unsuitable, unworthy men. Like too many women, we had both fallen into the trap of thinking we could heal damaged people. We learned too late that leopards don't change their spots. But we both felt on fine form once we regained our freedom. Ingrid and I get on well because we can talk for hours about girlie things like clothes and make-up, but we also love roughing it in the great outdoors.

'We're the best advertised single people in Britain!' I joked with Ingrid at one point that winter. We decided we might as well enjoy it for as long as it lasted.

But being single was absolutely no problem for me. I was planning some big new trips overseas and some tough new hikes at home; I was throwing myself into my work and social life. The very last thing I expected was to fall in love – but that's exactly what I did.

Chapter Nineteen
New Love

With Jonathan Ashman, it was third time very, *very* lucky. I knew nothing about it at the time, but we could have met many years ago. We *did* meet a few years ago. Then we finally got together in the spring of 2007.

You can't rewrite history and life right now could hardly be better. But how I wish I had seen Jonathan on that very first occasion! If we had spoken back then, I might never have fallen for Lembit – he would have been someone else's problem for all those years.

Here's the story of our various meetings. The time we might have met took place at Ladies Day at Royal Ascot back in the mid 1990s. I was wearing a vast and bizarre hat shaped like a sunflower to raise money and awareness for the Macmillan Cancer Support charity. It was a glorious, sunny day and I walked across the paddock to the photo-call. In front of me, had I only known it, was Jonathan. Apparently, I got within yards of him when three Welsh ladies approached me. They recognised me and stopped to say hello. We talked about the weather, of course, about Wales, of course, and then they asked if they could have photographs taken with me.

Three cameras appeared and we all had a bit of a giggle posing under my vast hat and swapping places so everyone could be in everyone else's shot. Then, when we said our goodbyes and the ladies turned to the left, I turned to my right and made my way to one of the enclosures.

Had I carried on walking in my previous direction, I would have passed directly in front of Jonathan. And he says he would have complimented me on taking the time to have so many photos taken with the Welsh ladies. Apparently, in the years ahead he told the story of me and my big hat at Ascot many times whenever people spoke about ill-mannered, ungrateful celebrities. 'They're not all like that,' he argued.

But back at the races I had turned right when I should have gone straight ahead. I missed out on meeting the man I now value so much. And what were the chances of my ever meeting him again?

Whatever they were, I beat the odds. The second time we were in the same place we did actually speak. It was at a launch party for the Wales Rally GB, Britain's round of the World Rally Championships at the beginning of March. Jonathan was in charge of the rally. A huge marquee had been set up in Cardiff and I was a guest of Russell Goodway, the leader of Cardiff City Council. It was a busy, noisy event and we had high hopes that it was going to put Wales firmly on the rally map. Peter Hain had worked really hard to ensure the event came to Cardiff in the first place.

Early on in the evening, Russell introduced me to Jonathan. I remember a flash of bright-blue eyes as we shook hands. We said a few words, I had a few more looks at those eyes, and then an assistant came over to take him away to deal with some crisis. It was the night before the big event and he had a thousand things to do to make sure everything went smoothly.

The third time we met was an even more tense affair; this time, though, the pressure was on me. Peter Hain was hosting a St David's Day dinner at the Welsh Office in London. My good friend David Goldstone and I walked into the room together and who should we – and the rest of the guests – see right in front of us? None other than Lembit Opik!

It was the first time we had seen each other since news of our split had broken. And it was totally unexpected. Again, it was a busy, noisy room, but it seemed to go silent, all except for a collective intake of breath as everyone waited to see what would happen next.

And what happened was that Lembit scarpered! He scuttled off to some side room without so much as looking at me. And if I believe in fate at all, then it stepped in at that moment. Peter took my arm and led me across to a corner of the room as far away from Lembit's bolthole as possible. 'Siân, I'd like you to meet my good friend Jonathan Ashman,' he said.

In every way Jonathan was to be my knight in shining armour – a knight with shining blue eyes. I remembered those eyes the moment he mentioned our previous meeting in Cardiff. We talked about how the rally had gone back then and how important events like that were for the local economy in Cardiff. He told me a bit about his role in World Touring Cars, which got us straight on to travel, one of my favourite subjects. Finally I know we talked about his daughter, who was doing a PPE at Oxford and was thinking about a career in the media. I told him of my time at Oxford and said she should give me a call if she ever wanted to come to ITN and see how our news and political teams worked. He wrote her name on a business card, handed it to me and that was it.

Much of the rest of that night is a blur. I talked to lots of different people – Peter Hain always has a varied and interesting crowd at his functions. But I wasn't always paying attention to the conversation. Despite myself, I couldn't stop looking around to see if Lembit might be lurking somewhere. In the back of my mind, I thought he might pounce to either insult me or beg me for forgiveness. Neither option would have surprised me, bearing in mind what he could be like when he'd been drinking. Fortunately, he was nowhere to be seen and I left the party unscathed.

The next night I was hosting a St David's Day party at the fabulous Odette's restaurant in Primrose Hill in North London. I'd invited about 50 of my friends to feast on the chef Bryn Williams's superb ncoctions. It was a relaxed, easy and lovely evening and ryone had a good time. A friend had turn th assumed was the owner of an art gallery and atted briefly.

Back in my flat I looked out over the skyline of North London. I always mentally run through all the people I have met at functions and mull over the day's events. I was happy at the success of our little St David's Day gathering. I thought about the man with the incredible blue eyes from the night before and I looked in my handbag to see if I still had his card. Then I got a shock. The first card I picked out came from the art gallery boss, though it turned out I had got his job description just a tiny bit wrong. He was the head of marketing for Nissan UK. When I had been asking him about his next exhibition he had been talking about the Geneva Motor Show. We had been at completely cross purposes all night! He must have thought I was a complete idiot.

As I laughed at myself and wondered if I should drop him a line to explain my bizarre line of questions I found another card. It was Jonathan's – though this confused me as well because he had written his daughter's name at the top of it. The whole thing had all the ingredients of a French farce with everyone getting increasingly confused over who was who.

The following day I sent Jonathan a text to say I had enjoyed meeting him. I put a kiss at the end. But then I do that to everyone. I'd do that to my bank manager if I ever felt called upon to text him.

I got a reply straight away.

'Let's meet up for coffee one morning,' he suggested.

'I don't do mornings,' I replied, trying to be funny.

So he suggested an afternoon.

We hit upon Tuesday, 6 March for coffee. But my diary wasn't entirely clear. This was the day of the Television and Radio Industries Club TRIC awards. As far as the public are concerned, these aren't as glamorous as the BAFTAs or the Oliviers, but the TRIC awards are special for one key reason: the votes are cast by your peers in the industry so the accolades matter. I had won TRIC's

Weather Presenter's award in 2005 and had been desperately proud, but I didn't think there was any chance I would win again so soon. I told Jonathan what was going on and then fired off another text.

'I'm not going to get it. If I don't, you can take me for coffee. But if I do – it's champagne!' I said.

The awards took place in the ballroom at the Grosvenor House Hotel on Park Lane in London. You don't get tipped off if you've won and so I got a complete surprise when my name was called. After collecting the award and saying a few words from the stage, I was whisked off for a series of interviews and meetings. I was in great company that year. Fiona Bruce won the Newscaster's award, Gary Lineker won Sports Presenter of the Year and good old Ant and Dec were TV Personalities of the Year. Richard Hammond, aka the Hamster, won a special award too.

And all the time I just wanted to be with Jonathan. But still the hurdles rose up ahead of me. Now we had missed our slot for an afternoon coffee I was committed to going to an early-evening NCH reception at the National Gallery. You can't let a charity down and so I got in my taxi, pulled out my phone and texted Jonathan to suggest a new plan.

'9pm at Harvey Nichols Bar?' I texted.

Some of the TRIC people had been talking about the bar and restaurant there earlier on and so it was the first place that sprang to mind when I tried to think of a new venue. Jonathan said yes, and so our first date was finally ready to roll.

When we arrived, it turned out that the TRIC guys were there in force, though we sat as far away from them as politeness would allow. They very kindly kept sending congratulatory drinks over to Jonathan and me. None of them was even touched – we were too busy talking.

It was the first night we had actually been sitting down together and able to talk properly; the first time we hadn't been at a noisy reception and drowned out by other voices. It was wonderful. We were the last to leave the bar, practically swept out by the cleaners. Best of all, in my mind, we were stone cold sober. We hadn't needed alcohol to make our words flow.

Jonathan, ever the gentleman, drove me home at midnight. After letting myself into my flat, I put my award down. I had been a bit embarrassed about carrying it around all night, and hadn't wanted Jonathan to think I was showing off when I arrived with it at Harvey Nics. But I hadn't known what else to do with the thing. And in the end it hadn't mattered. Jonathan had been so genuinely pleased for me, truly interested in what the award meant and why I had got it. After so long with a man who couldn't care less about my achievements, it was so utterly refreshing.

But when would I see this new man again? Jonathan had already told me how much he travels with his job and he was out of the country the next day.

I was so unused to dating. All my life I had been in long-term relationships so the singles game was a tricky one to play. My first challenge had been working out if Jonathan was even available. In one of our early conversations, I was crushed when he mentioned his daughter. That must mean he's married, I decided, so he's off limits. But then I picked up a few other conflicting clues.

We were texting each other a lot – and I enjoyed feeling like a teenager with a crush. And, like I say, I was fishing for information. The first clue came when Jonathan texted me after getting home, hungry, late one night.

'My fridge is bare,' he wrote.

Sounds like he's single, but you never know, I thought. I got my next clue as we tried to make our first coffee date. I'm a huge coffee snob – I have been so ever since my days at Bar Italia, Patisserie Valerie and Monmouth Coffee House in the West End when I was at the National Broadcasting School. In another text, Jonathan let slip: 'I have a coffee machine I never use.' I'm not sure why, but that screamed 'single' at me as well.

Anyway, for whatever reason when Jonathan was back from Brazil, I felt I had to be absolutely sure that he was single. He suggested meeting at his house for coffee the following afternoon.

'I don't go to people's houses without a reference,' I texted back, half-joking, half-serious. Jonathan got to work.

By total coincidence, a fellow Welshman, the opera singer Bryn Terfel, had lived in the basement of Jonathan's old house. Jonathan texted him (we were like lovesick teenagers at this point) and asked him to provide the required reference. Bryn replied to Jonathan with a message – in Welsh. So Jonathan had to take a leap of faith in forwarding it to me. Fortunately he was fine. Bryn gave his neighbour a ringing endorsement. I went round for coffee at four that afternoon. That evening we went out for dinner at Jacobs on Gloucester Road. The hours flew by. Once more I wasn't home till gone 2am the following morning.

NEW LOVE

Late night or no late night, meeting Jonathan was already doing something good to me – as Gaby Roslin was about to find out to her eternal embarrassment. I was on cloud nine about this wonderful new man when I headed off to film a celebrity-based charity edition of David Dickinson's *Real Deal* for ITV.

My good mood must have been pretty obvious. I was in the green room having a gossip and a catch-up with Toyah Willcox when Gaby walked in. 'Siân, things are obviously going well with you and Lembit – you look fantastic,' she said, as the whole room went silent.

It turned out the show was pretty much Gaby's first job since having her second baby at the end of the previous year. She hadn't been reading the gossip columns while she was at home being a mum and so my little crisis had passed her by. It was a useful way to put it into perspective. And the other message came to me loud and clear: if I did indeed look fantastic – thanks, Gaby – then it was because I was no longer with Lembit. It was because I had just met Jonathan. This was the kind of adult, grown-up, functioning relationship I needed. It was fantastic.

As if things couldn't get any better, Jonathan and I found we had something very important in common: Wales. His dad had been an amateur photographer who had taken some stunning landscape pictures for Great Western Railways, including some of the mid-Wales mountains I adored. So, in the spring of 2007, we decided to retrace some of his steps.

We started off on Cader Idris in South Snowdonia and then we headed to the magical Hafren Forest to go to the source of the River Severn. It is stunningly beautiful there and I suggested a great trek I knew well. We set off and Jonathan realised he had yet another connection to it: he had explored it several times when working on the Wales Rally GB circuit. After several days of hikes – in some pretty extreme weather – it was wonderful to pile back into the country cottage and relax. Trish was one of the first visitors to see us spend time there as a couple. She and Eric joined us for a weekend and made a comment I can't forget. 'This place is finally the love nest it always should have been, but never was,' she told me. One year on and counting, and it still is.

Of all people, I should be able to say that clouds have silver linings and one result of my brief spell in the headlines when I split with Lembit was that I got even more work than usual. As the offers came in, I thought back to that awful voice message Lembit had left after his father's funeral, and how different my life was just a year later: since I got my freedom back, I have done big corporate promotions for the likes of Vauxhall and Tesco. I've been flooded with offers to present various awards ceremonies and I've appeared on everything from *Ant and Dec's Saturday Takeaway* to the political programme *This Week*. In addition, I've presented film programmes on the new Film 24 channel, co-hosted an ITV2 series on the Welsh Assembly elections, done ads and even made a cartoon about a toy tiger.

Film 24 is a brilliant gig – the film-lover in me is in heaven. But I also get a thrill out of the whole production process. We film it in Pinewood and I can't believe I get paid to spend time there. I think of all the films that have

NEW LOVE

been made on those sound stages – from the 'Carry On' series to James Bond. Best of all, Jonathan has friends who live near by, so when he's around we get to combine my work with some extra socialising straight afterwards. Then we head up to the cottage in mid-Wales. It couldn't be more perfect.

At the end of 2007, I also had a chance to show off a new skill – or at least my attempt at it. I had been sent to Paris to learn the Can-Can from the girls at the Moulin Rouge. It was part of a show called *The Big Wedding* on Channel 4 in Wales, S4C. My role was to help take part in the hen night to end all hen nights – don't ask why, but this involved learning how to dance. I could hardly have had more fun and having a trip on the Seine in full dancer's regalia and stage make-up was something I'm unlikely to forget. Being 49 certainly wasn't going to stop me taking on new challenges!

Most amazing of all, being 49 didn't stop me being voted Rear of the Year in 2007 either. After I got over the shock, I was thrilled – though, as usual, I can always rely on my friends to keep my feet firmly on the ground. 'Of course you should be Rear of the Year, love,' Stifyn laughed. 'You were with one for long enough!'

Jokes apart, lining up alongside my male winner, sparky 26-year-old Lee Mead from *Joseph and the Amazing Technicolor Dreamcoat*, did feel pretty good. The awards help to promote the Beating Bowel Cancer charity and have been going for 25 years. I was easily the oldest winner they had ever had. In the past few years the award has gone to the likes of Charlotte Church, Denise van Outen and the singer Javine Hylton.

The organisers arranged a ceremony at the Dorchester Hotel in London in September 2007. Lee and I both had to bring a favourite pair of jeans and had the charity logo stamped on the pocket. There were two or three photographers in the room with us at the presentation and for a while we both thought that was it. Then Lee and I were led outside to one of the biggest media scrums I have seen in years. Who knew that things like Rear of the Year were still such big news? But then I know the headline writers had plenty of cheeky puns to put in their picture captions, so I guess we attracted more attention than normal.

For weeks afterwards, I seemed to take on the role of the iconic older woman. I don't think my agent has ever taken so many calls for other photo-shoots or programme ideas. One of the most exciting was a joint proposal for myself and Ingrid Tarrant: a production company wanted to take us to America to reprise the *Thelma and Louise* journey across the States by car! Neither of us could think the trekking anything more exciting. But I never assume any show will come off until the ink on the contract is dry. In the meantime, Ingrid and I did have one firm plan: we were doing a trek to the Rift Valley in Kenya to raise money for Marie Curie, so we were in serious training. I think the trekking was what gave me an award-winning rear in the first place.

I've never followed a strict exercise regime, had a personal trainer or been a slave to the gym: walking is something I adore and find immensely relaxing. I thrive on being busy in both my work and social life, so you could say that rushing around is my favourite workout! I feel truly blessed to have such an enthusiastic approach to life and am convinced that when you are in the right place mentally your energy levels are high. Getting the most out of every day is where my focus is and that really helps me to implement sensible habits. For example, I never drink coffee after six. I enjoy having a glass of wine or champagne, but I don't enjoy a hangover and therefore I limit the amount I drink and always counter the effects of alcohol by drinking lots of juice and water. I love freshly made juices and find them great for giving a mental and physical boost.

Throughout all of this, I had Jonathan in my corner – and that felt incredibly good. What meant the most, and what I never got from Lembit, was a sense of being in a team. We joined forces in life, rather than just existing in separate bubbles. Jonathan and I are constantly opening up and comparing our diaries – just like Ffion and William and all my other functional adult friends do. Even when we are apart, we text and speak constantly on the phone because we both want to know how our days were going. I loved extending my circle of friends to include Jonathan's. He did the same for me. I simply cannot believe I lived without such simple pleasures for so long.

Maybe I'm betraying my very faint-hearted feminist roots by saying it's also such a relief to be with a man who wants to help out around the house again. Jonathan wants to be part of my life. He's sharing, caring and considerate – and he makes my life run smoothly, and that's a wonderful thing after doing everything for myself for so long. I have always believed that good relationships should be about sharing life's load. You should want to help your partner out whenever you can. The feeling should be mutual. You should never be adding up the costs. Without wanting to wax too lyrical, Jonathan displays this support in so many ways. He's interested in my career, but there is no way he's threatened by it. And he also cares how I am perceived by others. Right from the start of our relationship he suggested I get my highly inaccurate Wikipedia entry updated, for example –I hadn't even bothered looking at it.

I think in the first six months of our relationship we spent more time together than Lembit and I would have done in six years! We went to Canada for the Montreal Grand Prix and then took a few weeks off afterwards to go walking and cycling around Nova Scotia. I loved Cape Breton, the lobster dinners and the wild scenery, with the fresh air of coastal Wales. We have also been to China, Hong Kong, Paris, Kenya, Tanzania, Valencia and Amsterdam, and as I'm determined to keep up my travel writing I'm hoping we will get plenty more destinations under our belts before long.

Throughout it all, I hope the weather remains the backbone of my career. I have never regretted leaving general reporting on World Wide Television News and turning to the weather at ITN. As far as I am concerned, weather has never been a stepping stone to anything else – it's a destination all of its own. And it becomes more interesting – and more important – all the time.

On a purely social level, it's never going to go away as a key topic of conversation. The weather affects so much of what we all do – from what we wear to how we feel. When Ceri and I talk on the phone, the first thing we do is discuss the weather in Paris and in London or Wales and what this means for our clothes. On a broader canvas, climate change really can't be ignored. My Met Office team and I see records broken all the time. The reports I give today are very different from those of a decade or more ago. Weather records are being broken on almost a monthly basis, or so it seems. Things are more volatile; it all matters more. But I can't predict how fast things might change or how worrying it may all become – I can only do what I am trained to do: to forecast the sunshine and the showers for the next few days. Then I keep my fingers crossed and hope for the best.

I do the same in my personal life now. When people ask me what I think will happen in my future, I joke that I'm a weather forecaster, not a soothsayer. But I do know one thing: in 2008 I'm feeling happier, more relaxed and more loved than I have in many years. I feel as if I have walked through a lot of storms. I know I didn't take always shelter from them as quickly as I should have, but I've learned from them. I'm confident about the future!

Chapter Twenty
Wedding Bells

As it turned out, I couldn't have wished for a more incredible or romantic autumn. It began with a trip to Africa – and it ended with my wedding in Wales.

In November I joined Jonathan on a trip to Kenya for the East African Classic Safari. The rally is an incredible mix of tradition and technology. All the cars have to be pre-1975 vehicles, though they have been totally re-built to go flat out on some of the bumpiest roads in the world. You really do need to be an enthusiast – and a rich one – to compete. As Jonathan was the chief steward of the rally we were in the thick of it from the off. The drivers have four days crossing the bush, one rest day then four more days of competition before reaching the finish line in Mombassa. Everyone stays in wonderful lodges along the way. It's Africa and it's a serious race. But these drivers don't need to rough it, which meant we didn't either.

I loved the easy camaraderie of the rally. The drivers all

want to win. But they help each other as well. It's sport the old-fashioned way. The only downside to the trip was the discovery that it's difficult to get a decent cup of coffee in Kenya. It seems that ground coffee is considered common. People show off by serving Nescafé. I wasn't impressed.

Jonathan and I spent the one rest day amid the incredible wildlife of Amboseli National Park. The peak of Mount Kilimanjaro disappeared into the clouds just beyond our lodge. It's one of the most beautiful sights in the world.

'Let's go and watch the sunset,' Jonathan said as we settled in. He swears he had no hidden agenda, but I'm not so sure.

We drove to a place called Observation Hill thinking it might be packed with tour groups. But it looked as if we might enjoy this view on our own. There was just one other vehicle in the car park, a converted Toyota that looked like something out of *Chitty Chitty Bang Bang*. The driver was a charming half German, half Australian engineer who was driving across Africa on the way to his next job. We chatted briefly as we passed and he offered us some wine. We shared a glass with him as the African sun started to dip. It was one of those relaxed and wonderful moments you can have when you are travelling.

It got better.

By the time the three of us had climbed to the observation point the clouds were lifting from Kilimanjaro. The sunset was a haze of reds, purples, oranges and golds. Our new friend, Stefan, took some great pictures of Jonathan and me. Then when he headed off to capture some other views, Jonathan put his arms around me and asked the question.

'Sian. Will you marry me?'

WEDDING BELLS

'Of course I will.'

Apparently that was my clear, if unromantic reply – I can't quite remember it myself. But I know that I didn't even need a second to think about it. Not one second.

When Stefan wandered back we didn't tell him that our lives had just changed. He took some more pictures for us – before and after, if you like. Then we waved him goodbye. The whole thing had been simple, powerful, emotional and wonderful. It was private. Just as our wedding would be.

Back in the lodge in Amboseli we sent a few texts back home with our news. But other than that we wanted to keep it a secret and not make a fuss – not least because Jonathan still had a rally to run. The next day disappeared in a haze of dust and laughter as we bounced over the roads to our next stop, Arusha. And it was there, quite by chance, that I found my beautiful engagement ring.

One of the rally sponsors had been talking about tanzanite, which is mined nearby. Some friends of his owned a mine and a jewellery store and he suggested we go over and take a look. For some reason I think I had expected that everything there would be a bit gaudy and tasteless. I couldn't have been more wrong. I found my perfect ring straight away. It's very simple and its colours seem to change by the moment. It will always remind me of the sunset on Mount Kilimanjaro.

The lovely Indian couple who owned Prima Jewels and the mine had another string to their bow. They also owned an Indian restaurant – so that's where we went for lunch to celebrate our purchase. It was there that Jonathan took the picture of me and my ring that went in the newspapers.

It's all a bit camp and silly. But it's the happiest snapshot I've ever seen.

Three days later we were back in Mombassa for the end of the rally. And there was still magic in the air. We picked the Tamarind, Mombassa's most romantic restaurant for dinner – and we were given the most romantic table, right on the edge of the terrace overlooking the shadows on the creek. It was as if the staff knew we had something special to celebrate. Neither of us could stop smiling as we ate – curried lobster with coconut rice. Everything was falling into place and felt right. Having needed three attempts to get Jonathan and me together, it seemed as if the fates weren't going to let us mess up now.

Back in Britain we wanted to be married as soon as possible. The utterly charming staff at Chelsea Old Town Hall said this would be 16 days after starting the paperwork. But would we find a venue at such short notice? As a girl I had said I wanted to be married in the fairytale surroundings of Portmeirion in Wales. Could that dream come true as well?

We rang up to see if the ceremony could happen the moment our licence came through – Sunday 30 December. The staff could do it, but they only had three rooms left for guests. It was another sign that it was all meant to be – because three rooms were all we needed. We made the booking then and there.

I'm not sure how many people saw my ring flashing as I did the Christmas weather on ITN in 2007. I was certainly aware of it every time I pointed to the maps. I also think I smiled more than usual on those Bank

Holiday forecasts. After all I knew my wedding day was just around the corner.

Sunday 30 December 2007 was my perfect day. It began with sunshine, it was filled with laughter and it ended with me in the arms of my husband.

The beam of sunlight flooded into our room in Portmeirion when Jonathan opened the curtains on our wedding morning. It set the tone for a wonderfully romantic day – I couldn't have forecast it better if I had tried.

The registrar for our ceremony was a lovely lady called Mrs Olwen Jones. She was waiting downstairs for us at noon – along with our tiny band of witnesses. Novello Noades and Stifyn Parri were mine, Bryn Terfel and Jonathan's friend Andy Millns were his. David Goldstone was in charge of the ring. There was a real completeness in Bryn being there – after all, he'd provided the text reference that inspired me to meet up with Jonathan in the first place.

In Portmeirion's Mirror Room our wedding was as simple, informal and relaxed as possible. We had plenty of laughs – Stifyn saw to that. But we also had some tears. My eyes filled up when David Goldstone produced a ring for Jonathan – the man who had always said he didn't want to wear one. I read out a short Native American poem about companionship and love. Then we all headed out for some group photos and then to the big round table of the beautiful private dining room. Ron Noades and Andy's wife Lalage were with us and what an eclectic bunch we were. Among other things we included an opera singer, a football club owner, a theatrical impresario, property developer and a rally co-driver. And we all had one thing in common: we all wanted to relax, laugh and celebrate this wonderful day.

It was dark when we finally said our goodbyes. Jonathan and I headed back to mid-Wales. He lit a fire and we cuddled up on the sofa with a plate of Welsh cheese. For the next week and half we saw other friends, went for long walks and just got ready for the next, magical chapter of our lives. It's not the end of my story; it's the start of a whole new one. I know now that this isn't a funny kind of love. It's real love. It's been worth waiting for.

Epilogue
Lessons Learned

For me, life is certainly never boring. There are always new adventures to be had and lessons to be learned. Some of those lessons along the way have been very painful ones, but, unless you experience the lows, you can never fully appreciate the highs. There's not much point in chalking up regrets in life when you can't go back and change things. But I do like to reflect on what I have learned from situations and how that might help me to handle things differently in the future.

With personal relationships, I feel that my values and my instincts have always guided me in the right direction. The minute I stepped into the unfamiliar territory and the world of Lembit Opik, I had my first real relationship casualty. Because I had no previous experience of a dysfunctional relationship and the emotional turmoil that comes with it, I missed all the early warning signs. With the benefit of hindsight, I can now see why conflict was inevitable. Lembit was very unconventional, whereas I am a very conventional girl at heart. Being punctual, reliable and giving a partner access to every area of my life is second nature to me.

I know that many people will read this book and wonder why it took me so long to end my relationship with Lembit. I often ask myself the same question, but in the heat of the moment it is difficult to have perspective on your circumstances. For me, it's not about defending the time it took me to leave Lembit, but coming to terms with and understanding why it took so long. In the process, I've learned a lot about myself and my attitude to relationships.

I also see that, while it's my nature to nurture, support and help the man in my life, I was also too inclined to try to fill in the gaps. Often I think of the analogy of two people fitting together like a jigsaw puzzle, complementing each other and completing the picture. That's very different from trying to make a person whole, like a kind of joining-the-dots exercise. If what you are seeing are fatal flaws in a person, you will never have a happy, healthy relationship. When something isn't working, I have learned not to make it my sole responsibility to fix it.

I've come across people who seem to conduct their relationships in a kind of isolation. They go through the motions, but you get the impression they are not really tuned into their partner and they are more concerned about having their own needs met. I've never been like that and have no desire to be. I'm proud of my passionate and generous nature. I'm very much an all or nothing person. I don't do half-hearted friendships or relationships.

LESSONS LEARNED

I accept the fact that I run the risk of being taken advantage of, but I've considered the alternative. I could become mistrusting towards others, hold back more and make far less effort than I do, basically become someone I'm not. For me that would be a very grim option because the vast majority of people in my life do live up to my high expectations. Their capacity to give back is limitless and I have a real sense of synchronicity about those relationships. They flow beautifully and I would not benefit from those wonderfully warm people in my life by holding back.

Being on the receiving end of an emotional rollercoaster is a very hurtful experience. I would swing from immense sadness to anger. Lembit had a knack of making me feel he needed me. I don't think it was a case of feeling flattered so much as being too inclined to allow myself to feel responsible for him. While his behaviour was often inconsiderate and thoughtless, I never wanted to sell myself short by matching it. But I did want to have my say about what happened.

I certainly don't see myself as a martyr or some tragic victim who lost out on love. I'm not a quitter by nature and never shy away from a challenge. That has a lot to do with my upbringing; my parents always taught me to use my brain and said you have to work hard for anything that is worth achieving in life. I was never part of the instant-gratification generation. Equally, the desire to be famous was not at the top of my career list, as it is for many young people today.

My upbringing also instilled in me the importance of consistency in a person's nature. Both my parents were great advocates of being strong-minded freethinkers. They

279

encouraged us to educate our minds, form our own opinions, but have the ability to back up those opinions. They would never have entertained bad behaviour or bad manners. I was always taught to be accountable for my behaviour. That helped me to develop not only a greater awareness for other people but also a respect. Investing in people and relationships has played a significant role in my life from childhood.

Today I can smile to myself when I think about how Lembit would try to convince me his way was right and mine was wrong, and how, if he really thought it was such a good option, he didn't team up with someone like himself. I have no desire to pursue a hedonistic lifestyle. Putting myself out for others has never felt like a compromise, in my view: when you care about someone, doing your bit brings its own rewards. I love doing things for Jonathan and there's never any sense of effort because he goes out of his way to do things for me too. It feels great to be back in the ebb and flow of life and a million miles away from the chaos and confusion that surrounded my previous relationship.

I can see now that, with previous personal relationships, they continued after the romance had run its course. They were cemented by a strong bond of friendship and our lives in many ways had become intertwined. There was never a dramatic final break-up, no heated arguments or words of recrimination. A mutual respect and consideration always remained intact. If either person needed support or had a crisis, there was never any question about being there for each other. I guess I came to expect that and very much considered it the norm.

LESSONS LEARNED

Emotionally destructive or dysfunctional relationships are not apparent from day one. They weave their way into your life. Gradually, my relationship with Lembit and my role as a caring supportive partner evolved into the role of someone who was trying to fix their partner. While I knew for a long time that my love affair with Lembit was well and truly over, I was completely locked into trying to salvage something from it.

Turning my back on Lembit when his father and brother died was not something I could do. My efforts may not have been appreciated but they make me the person I am. I can live with being a soft touch and having a compassionate nature. I can also live with the fact I gave him too much credit and thought the good guy in him would win through in the end.

Contending with the stark contrast of the sober Lembit and the Lembit who was less so drove me to utter despair. I would watch a talented, passionate man deliver a wonderful speech, then receive a phone call in the middle of the night from a person I didn't recognise. I would listen to the illogical, erratic ramblings of someone who sounded like they had lost their grip on reality.

One of the things I have always hated about both alcohol and drugs – though I never saw Lembit anywhere near drugs – is how they hijack a person. They seem to rob them of good qualities and bring out the darker side we all have within us. Being in a relationship with someone who is a heavy drinker is like having three people in the relationship. The alcohol becomes the mistress you can never compete with. Believe me, I put up a fight for the good guy.

Time and time again, I would try to confront Lembit about his heavy drinking. I was almost consumed by wanting to save him from himself and the dreadful demons that are fuelled by alcohol. I'd never had any previous experience of the levels of denial that exist in those situations. I felt an enormous sense of outrage and helplessness as I witnessed the good qualities in Lembit fading into the background. It was never my intention to turn a personal relationship into a crusade, but that's exactly what happened. I was sucked in and it took me a long time to realise how much I was jeopardising my own happiness and sanity.

It's one thing to be there for someone, but I've learned you can't fight someone's corner when they have given up on themselves and refuse to acknowledge they have a problem. Lembit was comfortable surrounding himself with people who never questioned him or took exception to his rowdy drunken behaviour. My confrontations with him fuelled a growing resentment. The more I tried to help, the more resentment I encountered. Eventually, I realised that however much I wanted to be able to walk away with a friendship, the foundations for that had been well and truly bulldozed.

Like I said, hindsight is not something you have at the time. However, you can benefit from it and use it to bounce back from a very difficult experience. I'm sure I will never make the same mistake again and I won't allow the experience to dent my optimistic approach to relationships.

I'm a firm believer that life always conspires to support your beliefs. Perhaps that fuels my optimistic outlook that there are lots of good times ahead. I might sound like I'm stating the obvious, but no one has a problem-free life. There will always be the unpredictable problems that arise and the sadly more predictable ones such as bereavement. As for the day-to-day challenges of life, I now feel that I can take them in my stride and never feel jaded or worn down by them!